100 Ideas for Primary Teachers

Homework

Jenna Lucas

B L O O M S B U R Y

LONDON · OXFORD · NEW YORK · NEW DELHI · SYDNEY

Bloomsbury Education
An imprint of Bloomsbury Publishing Plc

50 Bedford Square
London
WC1B 3DP
UK

1385 Broadway
New York
NY 10018
USA

www.bloomsbury.com

Bloomsbury is a registered trademark of Bloomsbury Publishing Plc

First published 2017

British Library Cataloguing-in-Publication Data
A catalogue record for this book is available from the British Library.

ISBN:
PB 9781472944757
ePub 9781472944726
ePDF 9781472944764

Library of Congress Cataloging-in-Publication Data
A catalog record for this book is available from the Library of Congress.

10 9 8 7 6 5 4 3 2 1

Typeset by Newgen Knowledge Works (P) Ltd., Chennai, India
Printed and bound by CPI Group (UK) Ltd, Croydon, CR0 4YY

This book is produced using paper that is made from wood grown in managed, sustainable forests. It is natural, renewable and recyclable. The logging and manufacturing processes conform to the environmental regulations of the country of origin.

To view more of our titles please visit
www.bloomsbury.com

Contents

Acknowledgements

Firstly, I would like to pay a huge acknowledgement and thanks to all the teachers who have inspired me with their own ideas, offered their own words of wisdom and played their own parts in developing my classroom teaching. At the time of writing this, my very first head teacher, Chris Dursley, is preparing to retire. We often think of the impact we have as teachers on the children we work with, and quite rightly so, but I want to thank Chris for the impact she had on *me* in my first three years of teaching: for the opportunities and the encouragement, and of course for the good reference when I moved on! I also want to give a special mention to a group of teachers I haven't actually worked in a school with, but whom I speak to every day, and who continually inspire me, challenge me and, undoubtedly, make me laugh – thank you to the Primary Rocks crew: Gaz Needle, Graham Andre, Rob Smith, Sophie Merrill, Bryn Goodman, Ang Goodman, Tim Head, Leah Sharp and Rich Farrow. You genuinely do all rock!

Many of the ideas in this book have been developed from conversations with, or blogs written by, other people. Massive thanks to Ross Morrison McGill, for sharing Takeaway Homework; to Stephen Lockyer, who inspires so much of what I do in the classroom (and gave some good advice regarding writing over a beer in Alton – thank you!); and to Martyn Reah, who set me on the path to well-being and, in particular, developing it with the students – Chapter 1 is dedicated to you! Thanks also to Julia Skinner, creator of the '100-word challenge' – my pupils LOVE this.

I'd also like to thank Miriam Davey, my wonderful editor, who invited me to write my first book (definitely something ticked off the bucket list!) and has been nothing short of amazing. Thank you for your patience, encouragement, suggestions and for always being at the end of an email when I've needed you!

And last, but by no means least, thank you to my family, who I simply could not have written this book without. To my mum and dad, who bought my first typewriter – I finally got my name in print! Thank you for your interest, your support and the hours you give to helping me with childcare so I can have my cake and eat it! Thanks to my husband, Jim, for the endless cups of tea and for always telling me to 'go for it'. The best co-parent I could ask for. And of course, the biggest thanks of all to my two bubs, Grace and Jack, who inspire me daily; it is all for you.

Introduction

Homework has always been a rather contentious subject. Debate often falls around whether there is any real point to it, particularly in the primary years. Does it genuinely have any impact on a child's learning and progress, or is it simply an add-on which only increases teacher workload and causes tensions at home? Conversations within staffrooms and among social media groups highlight teachers' concern over setting homework, and I often hear parent friends discuss what homework *they* have to complete that weekend!

However, despite of these concerns, homework remains policy for many primary schools and, if done well, can be of real benefit to all concerned. Homework should support children in their learning, reinforce what is happening in the classroom with real-life contexts and refrain from being too onerous a task for parents, children or teachers.

The main thing I ask of parents is that they read with their children. Every day. Right through the primary years. This, and practising spellings, times tables and number bonds, will stand children in good stead. Other homework tasks, if carefully thought through, can enhance classroom teaching and promote pupil well-being. The homework should be of benefit to both the children and the teachers!

This book is a collection of ideas, borne from the desire to engage children in their homework (or home learning as it is often referred) in a way that supports in-class learning and doesn't result in additional marking. The ideas move away from the traditional worksheets to a range of suggestions designed to reinforce and extend learning across the curriculum. I say 'suggestions' because I am all too aware that each school setting is different, as is each teacher and each class of 30-something pupils – so some ideas might need adapting, picking and mixing, allowing you to add your own pizzazz.

Set homework expectations from the start and ensure that children, and therefore parents, are clear on what they need to do. Working *with* parents will make a significant difference. Chapter 1 contains ideas to support the well-being of children and families. In my experience, this type of homework, even if set alongside weekly spelling or reading tasks, is always valued. I hope the ideas in this book will help inspire you to set homework that has an impact and is worthwhile; to the children, their families and you!

How to use this book

This book includes quick, easy, practical ideas and guidance for you to dip in and out of, to help you plan some exciting and worthwhile homework activities for the children in your class.

Each idea includes:

- a catchy title, easy to refer to and share with your colleagues
- a quote from a practitioner, parent or child describing their experience that has led to the idea
- a summary of the idea in bold, making it easy to flick through the book and identify an idea you want to use at a glance
- a step-by-step guide to implementing the idea.

Each idea also includes one or more of the following:

Teaching tip

Practical tips and advice for how and how not to run the activity or put the idea into practice.

Taking it further

Ideas and advice for how to extend the idea or develop it further.

Bonus idea ★

There are 49 bonus ideas in this book that are extra exciting, extra original and extra interesting.

Share how you use these ideas and find out what other practitioners have done using #100ideas.

STUDENT 5 A DAY

Part 1

Student 5 a day

'The best homework we get!'

'Student 5 a day' homework is a termly list of suggested activities that incorporate the five ways to well-being originally listed by the New Economics Foundation (NEF).

Teaching tip

Ensure the suggested activities include a range from the five strands so that children have a choice to pick from. Not every activity will suit every family!

Ever mindful of the impact of homework on home life, I introduced 'student 5 a day' at my school, with the help of the school council. Being involved with Twitter's #teacher5aday community (founded by Martyn Reah, a deputy headteacher), I wanted to think about how we promote pupil well-being along the same lines, and so the elements of notice, learn, exercise, volunteer and connect have become a regular part of termly homework. Each term, the school council devises a list of ten suggested activities that can be completed at home to promote whole-family well-being. Each class councillor then delivers these to their classmates, where the children are encouraged to complete the activities at home as well-being homework.

Some of the suggestions from my own school include:

- draw a wild landscape
- learn to count to ten in another language
- find things in nature to make every colour of the rainbow
- take part in a sport outside of school
- make your own bed
- leave a note for somebody to say thank you
- set the table for dinner.

There are infinite possibilities of ideas but what makes it particularly special is that the homework is also set by the children. The ideas belong to them!

Bonus idea ★

Ask the pupils to record any well-being homework they have completed or any new hobbies they may have found as a result. Hold a class or school celebration each term where well-being at home is applauded.

All about me

'I got to find out so much about the children in my class.'

If you belong to any social media teaching groups you will be familiar with the sharing of lesson ideas and displays. During the end of the summer term, my social media feeds fill up with 'all about me' activities, in preparation for meeting a new class. One of my favourite activities for getting to know a new bunch of faces is the 'all about me' bag.

Provide a paper bag at the start of the summer holidays or in the first week of the new school year. The bag can be personalised by the children, and should come back to school containing three to five items that can be used to share some interesting information with the teacher and new class. These often include small items (usually related to a hobby or perhaps the child's faith), photos and certificates.

Back in school, the bags can initially be shared in pairs, and then in groups. To prepare for this, I ask the children to practise their short presentations at home. Speaking and listening skills are developed, as children can introduce the items of their partner's bag to the rest of the group (a great way of getting the children to really take on board what they are hearing!).

This homework task not only provides a great opportunity for an initial speaking and listening assessment, but gives a real insight into the pupils' lives beyond school.

Teaching tip

Before the children talk about the items in their own bags, ask other pupils to infer what the items can tell us about each person.

Teaching tip

Create your own 'all about me' bag, sharing some information about your own life out of school. A great way to build relationships with your pupils!

Bonus idea ★

Display one anonymous item at a time. Can the children work out who it might belong to and give reasons why?

Home help

'Getting the kids to help around the house teaches them responsibility, as well as a few life skills!'

Helping out around the house is beneficial to both children and their families. Age-appropriate chores encourage responsibility and independence and promote a sense of family teamwork!

Teaching tip

Parents can be invited to write a small comment in the children's home/ school diaries, listing some of the chores undertaken.

Taking it further

Ask the children to keep a timetable of the chores they complete and when; this could be kept on a regular basis.

Bonus idea ★

Ask the children to create a 'how to' guide for younger children. This works particularly well after a residential trip, and can link with instructional writing: *How to make a bed*, *How to set a table*.

One of the main issues parents have with homework is the impact it has on family time. During my daughter's home visit before starting school, I remember her teacher asking that I help to prepare her for school life by encouraging her to pack away after herself and scrape her own plate after meals (an essential for when she would receive hot lunches). Hearing this as 'homework' from her teacher made a real difference; it was no longer a nag from mum!

I can recall several school residential trips where there has always been at least one child truly incapable of making up a bed. I soon learnt to mention this in the information evenings prior to the visit, asking parents to practise a few housekeeping skills, like making a bed, using cutlery and folding clothes.

Setting occasional 'home help' homework encourages children to play their part at home. Some suggestions (depending on the age of the children in your class) include:

- put dirty clothes into the laundry basket
- set the table or prepare lunch
- wash up/load the dishwasher
- make the bed and tidy their bedroom
- help wash the car
- help fold tea towels
- water the plants
- put the rubbish out.

Run for it

'As a family, it was so enjoyable to go for a 15-minute jog. It beats the battle over completing a worksheet any day!'

With childhood obesity on the rise, schools are being pressured more than ever to promote exercise and well-being amongst pupils. Regular PE lessons and seeking opportunities to take learning outside can support children with general fitness, but why not set it as homework too?

Over the last couple of years, I have really got into running. My family are regulars at the local Park Run and I can honestly say that the benefits have not only been physical but mental as well. Running is great because pretty much any child can put on a pair of trainers and get outside – for free! Setting it as homework encourages families to get outside and exercise and can also support curriculum learning, as well offering general health benefits.

Ask the children to run one mile (in a safe place, accompanied by an adult) or however long you think appropriate for the age of the children you teach.

- Younger children can describe how they felt during and after the run. What did they notice happening to their bodies? (Breath quickening, heart racing, feeling warmer.) Did they feel good after the run?
- Older children can locate where they ran on a map. What route did they take?
- Record the time taken to run a certain distance. Can they beat that time? Give the time in seconds, or minutes and seconds.
- Record their pulse rate before and after running. What do they notice? What do they think is happening?
- Keep an exercise journal, recording the different types of exercise they do.

Teaching tip

A brisk walk or gentle jog around the playground on a regular basis is a good way to lead up to such homework.

Taking it further

Inspire the children with videos of some our country's runners and athletes. Create a culture of celebrating exercise!

Taking it further

To make the homework really purposeful, discuss why exercise is so good for us. What are the physical and mental health benefits?

Emotional expressions

'Talking about what can trigger certain emotions helped us to recognise and deal with them.'

Being a child isn't always plain sailing. Many children struggle with their emotions, and are not always confident discussing them in class. Encouraging children to discuss how they feel — particularly with somebody they trust at home — can be the ideal way to reflect on different situations and the emotions that may arise as a result.

Taking it further

Discuss ways to deal with more difficult emotions, like embarrassment or anger. Return to school with some suggestions to be shared with classmates.

I suspect that it is probably rare that I send a text message without an accompanying emoji these days. On occasion, my reply to somebody only requires an emoji, usually the one with crying tears of laughter! Sites like Pinterest are full of examples of how these emojis can be used in the classroom, from creating story picture maps to exit slips used to inform assessment for learning. Looking at the emojis and what they represent can be a useful way of exploring our emotions, and the events or circumstances that might cause these.

Provide children with a sheet of different emoji expressions (examples are readily available online). At home, ask the children to sit with an adult or someone they feel comfortable with to discuss each emoji. What feeling does each emoji show? List the different emotions and take it in turns to say a sentence beginning with 'I feel . . .', using one of the emotions and a situation to complete the sentence. For example, 'I feel sad when I am left out in the playground' or 'I feel nervous when we have a test'.

Bonus idea ★

Ask children to consider their own facial expressions and body language when they feel a certain way. Can they create their own emojis to express these feelings?

Random acts

'No act of kindness, however small, is ever wasted.' Aesop

On a recent residential trip with our ten- and eleven-year-olds, my deputy head set a challenge one morning, asking the children to look out for any acts of kindness from their classmates. That same evening, snuggled up with hot chocolate and bourbon biscuits, we shared what was, for me, one of the best parts of the whole trip, as the children (and staff) told their stories of a friend being kind. Experiences like this are what make teaching so fulfilling.

Highlighting acts of kindness and suggesting possible 'acts' is a good way to get things started, and an opportunity to discuss the effects of being kind, for both the student and the teacher. But referring to it regularly and looking out for it in day-to-day life means it becomes so much more than an annual token gesture.

Provide a list of suggested acts of kindness for children to take home. These should be easy enough for the children to complete at home or around school, and families should be encouraged to get involved too! Examples might include:

- hold the door open for someone
- ask a family member how their day was
- share a game or toy
- pay someone a compliment
- comfort someone who is feeling down
- send a thank-you note.

To ensure these don't just become a one-off gesture, stick a copy of some suggested acts of kindness into the children's homework books or folders. Each week, ask the children to note down or highlight an act of kindness they have given or received. Reflecting on these can provide a great start-of-the-day activity or warm-up to a circle time session.

Taking it further

A whole school display or assembly can really raise the profile of acts of kindness and keep it high on the agenda.

Bonus idea ★

During the month of December, or any last week of term, share a list of random acts of kindness across the school, with a different act on each day. Getting the whole school community on board helps to raise spirits during that final hurdle, and works as a great alternative to an advent calendar.

Job application

'The classroom jobs have never been so popular.'

Children thrive when given responsibilities in school. A set of classroom jobs that require careful application mean the new roles won't be taken lightly!

Taking it further

Badges are available for many school roles, such as school councillor, sports leader or librarian, but why not get the children to make their own to wear throughout the year with pride?

This is an ideal homework task for the very start of the academic year but can follow at the start of each term as well. Create a jobs advertisement page, listing all of the jobs to be carried out in the classroom. These can range from watering the classroom plants to representing the entire class at the school council.

For homework, ask the children to write their letter of application, stating which job role they are applying for and why they are the most suitable person for that role. This can link to learning in persuasive writing. Parents or siblings can even provide a reference! It might be useful to provide a sample letter, modelling what is expected, including standards of spelling, grammar and punctuation.

Back in school, some of the roles may require the children to make a short speech to the class, such as those that will require a class vote.

Others may need to face a couple of basic interview questions, in order to find out the children's experience of washing paint pallets or handing out letters!

Once the children feel they have earned their roles, they are likely to take them on with pride and endeavour to be a success!

Thank you

'Appreciation is a wonderful thing. It makes what is excellent in others belong to us as well.' Voltaire

Encouraging children to give thanks is not only about being polite, but also about improving their own well-being as well as that of others.

During a visit to a school in Toronto several years ago, a display board caught my attention. It was an appreciation board filled with messages of thanks from students and teachers.

The NEF listed 'to give' as one of five steps to well-being. Taking time to do something for someone else is believed to increase our own happiness, and a simple thing like saying 'thank you' becomes more than just good manners!

Remembering those two simple words is often something that many children (and, dare I say, adults) need reminding of. I am well aware of my own feelings when I take the time to say thank you to someone and make them smile. Although this may seem a very simple, courteous gesture, which we should expect from everyone, setting it as a homework task will instil it further . . . and spread lots of good feeling!

How you set this, and what you expect from it is up to you, and will depend on the children you teach. Younger children can be encouraged to simply say thank you and explain why, perhaps drawing a picture of what they are thankful for. Older children can write a letter of thanks to somebody, explaining why they are grateful and the difference it has made.

This homework links well with PSHE lessons or during a Random Act of Kindness week. Children could also think of a friend or adult in school to thank.

Teaching tip

Model appreciation in the classroom. Ask the children to write post-it thank you notes to their peers. These can be displayed on an appreciation board and taken home at the end of the week.

Bonus idea ★

Appreciation is a great theme for a class assembly. Set the homework just beforehand and you will have a tonne of material for the class to share.

Moral dilemmas

'Intelligence is what you use when you don't know what to do.' Jean Piaget

Moral dilemmas, or questions to get the children (and their families) thinking, are not only fun as a homework task, but also support a range of generic skills, including listening, hypothesising, persuading and reasoning.

Taking it further

Ask the children to write their own moral dilemmas to share with the class once back in school. These can lead to really interesting debating sessions.

Present a moral dilemma or a 'thunk' (see *Thunks* by Ian Gilbert for lots of examples) as Talking homework (see Idea 91), to be discussed or considered at home. The task can take place as a family discussion, exploring different possible options, or the child can mind-map the options with likely consequences, before making a decision.

The Internet is full of great examples of moral dilemmas that can be printed and sent home, or put on the class webpage or blog. Examples include:

- You leave a shop realising you have been given too much change. Outside the shop, a homeless person is asking passers-by for any loose change. What options do you have? What do you choose to do?
- Your friend draws a picture of you for your bedroom wall that you really don't like. What are your options? What do you choose to do?
- Your teacher wants to know who smashed a window or the entire class will be punished. You know who broke the window. What are your options? What do you choose to do?

Empathy glasses

'Empathy: the ability to share and understand the feelings of another.'

Asking children to don their empathy glasses not only encourages empathy, but can support inference and deduction skills as well.

In *Zero Degrees of Empathy*, Simon Baron-Cohen says, 'empathy is like a universal solvent. Any problem immersed in empathy becomes soluble.' Like many life skills, he believes that empathy can be improved with practice.

Teachers of the 2000s (and many still) will all know the Department for Education's SEAL (Social and Emotional Aspects of Learning) materials. These were packs of books and resources that became the foundation of many PSHE lessons. In some schools, they still are. One of the best resources that came with this pack, in my opinion, is the photo pack. The pack was made up of eighty photo cards showing a range of scenarios, but the facial expressions and body language of the people within the pictures were superb for prompting discussion about our different emotions and possible causes.

It is useful to practise these skills in school prior to sending any pictures home. Study a picture and model the questions we might ask about what we can see.

- What can we see happening?
- Who is in the picture?
- How is the person feeling? How can we tell?
- When have we felt like this?

The task can take place as a family discussion or the child can thought-shower some words to describe the picture and what is happening. It is also useful for the children to ask questions about the picture, leading on from in-class modelling.

> **Bonus idea** ★
>
> Use pictures from newspapers or magazines of 'papped' celebrities. Ask the children to consider body language and facial expressions to empathise. A great example is the very famous photo of the little girl with her head on the desk as David Cameron speaks to her!

11

LITERACY

Part 2

What can you hear?

'Everybody, stop and listen.'

Early stages of learning to read include identifying sounds. As children grow, taking time to listen to the sounds around them can also be of huge value.

Teaching tip

Collect examples of the sounds that the children heard and write a class poem in the style of Roger McGough's *The Sound Collector*.

I regularly do this activity with my own children, as well as those I teach. There is something extremely therapeutic about just listening and, actually, this is a skill that many children need time to work on.

As their homework task, ask the children to spend ten minutes sitting down outside. This can be in their garden, at a local park or anywhere else they might be visiting. The challenge is to sit in silence and just *listen,* noting down at least ten things they hear. This could include a dog barking, a passing car, the squeaking of a swing or a squawking seagull.

Younger children can work on identifying initial sounds and labelling pictures of what they have heard. Older children could develop this by describing the sounds made: the *siren* of a police car; the *whistle* of the wind.

Can the children group the noises they hear? They might consider natural and man-made sounds, or relaxing sounds compared with more alarming ones.

Taking it further

Using picture stimuli, ask the children to imagine what they might hear if they were there. This can support descriptive writing – in particular, setting the scene through 'show, not tell'.

Listening activities are a good way of encouraging mindfulness. By sitting calmly, even for a few minutes, children can focus on their breathing, collect their thoughts and take time out from general busy-ness. It can also lead to some thoughtful discussions, as the pupils notice and ask questions about the things they can hear.

Rhyme it!

'This really helps me to see the ways we can spell different words with the same sounds.'

Learning rhymes starts at an early age. Many children start school equipped with the ability to recall their favourite rhymes. Once children start writing, knowing rhymes can really help with their spelling.

Early Years: Providing rhyming pictures is a great way to get children, particularly before they are writing, to identify the sounds of words. Pictures of CVC (consonant–vowel–consonant) words that can be cut out and stuck together encourage the children to say the words aloud and recognise the patterns.

Ages 5–7: As children get slightly older, give them one word – for example, 'chair' – and ask them to list as many rhyming words as possible. Spelling detectives can try to find some items in their homes that rhyme with the given word *(hair, highchair, square, nightwear, teddy bear, underwear)*. Some children will start to recognise that the 'air' sound can be spelt many different ways.

Ages 7–11: The poem *'Seeing is Definitely Not Believing'*, by Josie Whitehead, is a fantastic poem to share with older children. It really highlights the fact that sounds are often written using different spelling patterns. Using the website www.rhymezone.com, children can write their own verse, playing with language and spelling!

> **Teaching tip**
>
> Ask the children to share the words they listed at home. Collect the rhyming words and group them, according to their spelling pattern, and display on a class chart. This is a great way to support a weekly spelling focus.

Bookworms

'Reading is a vital life skill and it is important we encourage a love of reading in kids from a young age.' James Patterson

Making time for the class reading book is essential in any primary classroom. Homework tasks linked with a book help to further bring the story alive.

Reading with the children is my absolute favourite part of the school day – especially their facial expressions as they hang off every word, and their groans as the bell rings to signal home time. Quality reading books, and a shared passion from the teacher, make this possible. Homework activities that can build on the love of a good book, and provide opportunities for further exploration bring great value back to the classroom.

A favourite of mine has always been *Flour Babies* by Anne Fine. Ask children aged nine and above to create their own flour baby (this is the fun bit) and care for it, just like a real baby, for at least one week. It is important that they also keep a diary as, this way, they can really relate to and empathise with the book's characters. This is always a memorable homework activity!

Other activities can link around 'What would you do?' When reading *Kensuke's Kingdom*, by Michael Morpurgo, I asked the children to think about what they would have spent the money on and why Michael's dad might have chosen a yacht.

At the end of any book, it's good to ask the children to write a short review that could be shared on a site like Amazon. This provides an audience and a purpose, rather than a homework sheet that will simply be stuck in a folder.

Desert Island Discs

'What five things would you take if you were moving away?'

Desert Island Discs **is a weekly Radio 4 programme, where guests are invited to choose eight recordings, a book and a luxury item that they would take if they were to be cast away on a desert island.**

This homework activity is great for leading to discussion back in class, and links well with books like *Holes* by Louis Sachar, *Treasure Island* by Robert Louis Stevenson and *Kensuke's Kingdom* by Michael Morpurgo.

Ask children to look around at home and choose five items that they would take with them, should they be leaving their homes for a while. The answers that the children return to school with will vary, but always lead to a great discussion as to what gives an object value. Encourage children to justify their choices. This can lead to inference and deduction activities as we work out what the chosen items tell us about a certain person. Children should prepare some open questions beforehand to find out more about a partner's chosen items.

- Tell me about . . .
- Explain why . . .
- How would being without it affect you?

Discussions could provide an excellent basis for a philosophy session. Ask the children to consider what makes something valuable.

Taking it further

Encourage the children to get inside the minds of the characters they are reading about. What items would a particular book character choose to take with them? Why? Activities like this can be particularly useful for providing evidence in reading assessments.

Bonus idea ★

Send the children home with a list of objects. Who do the objects belong to and why?

Should have taken that left turn at Albuquerque

'Miss, I can still spell Albuquerque!'

There are some words, particularly those long, polysyllabic words, that so many children struggle to get to grips with. The 'Albuquerque' method, once learnt, can be used to learn and remember any spelling.

Taking it further

Provide the children with a list of high-frequency words or those that appear on statutory words lists. Ask children to learn these words through the Albuquerque method (or whichever name you choose to use!) and test regularly in school. The more often the children recall the spellings, the more likely they are to apply them correctly within their writing.

1. With the pupils, say the word aloud to find how many syllables it has. In the case of Albuquerque, four. Fold a long strip of paper into four sections; one for each syllable.
2. Take two different coloured pens. With the first colour, ask the pupils to write the letters of the first syllable in the first section of the strip of paper.
3. Orally repeat the letters whilst looking at them. Draw the letters in the air with your finger. Chant 'A . . . L' a few times.
4. Fold that piece behind and ask the pupils to take their second coloured pen and write the letters of the second syllable.
5. Repeat through the next three syllables (or through as many syllables as are in your chosen word). Focus on one section at a time, and then the whole word. Play with the word, spell the letters in the third syllable, the first, spell the word backwards. Have a bit of fun with it.
6. Ask volunteers to write the word up on the board and be amazed at how every child can now spell 'Albuquerque'!

This technique can be applied to any polysyllabic word that the pupils are struggling with. Once the method has been practised a few times, it can be taken on independently as homework.

TV script

'Guess what . . . I have to watch TV for my homework!'

Well, we might as well get some benefits from the children watching TV. Watching a scene and turning it into a script reinforces playscript features learnt at school, and allows the children to see their favourite movies or TV programmes in a new light.

Ask the children to select a scene from a favourite film, or a TV programme that they are able to pause. Using the features of a playscript that they have learnt in school, this homework gives the children the opportunity to practise further.

The children need to include cast members, setting and stage directions, as well as who says what and how.

When learning about direct speech, the children can write out a conversation from a favourite film or programme, showing what is said in inverted commas, with a description of the character's actions and emotions. Use of 'show not tell' can also be practised here.

An alternative option is to create a comic strip (see Idea 55). Ask the children to pause the show at certain points and recreate it on paper. Alternatively, draw a picture of a character at a certain point with a thought bubble, speech bubble and a heart bubble (to show feelings).

It is worth discussing the power of drama with the children, as well as the techniques used by an actor to convey the story.

Taking it further

Homework can be shared and evaluated when back at school, and even acted out. What makes it effective? What could be improved?

Pop grammar

'She has sung that bit with the wrong subject–verb agreement! It should be "You were", not "You was".'

'Pop grammar' works similarly to peer marking, but uses the work of a songwriter instead of the children's classmates. Playing 'teacher', children can mark and correct the lyrics of their favourite stars – a great activity for older primary children!

Taking it further

Provide the children with a printout of their favourite celebrities' tweets and ask them to fix that SPaG! It seems that footballers, pop singers and TV presenters could all do with a little help!

I really enjoy teaching grammar – the children in my class will happily testify to this. Unpicking the different parts of the spoken word is really interesting and I am always learning! Constantly on the lookout for new and engaging spelling, grammar and punctuation (commonly known as SPaG) ideas, I openly pinched Stephen Lockyer's spagalicious suggestion, posted on the Staffrm blogging site, which my children now know as 'pop grammar'.

After modelling an example in class using Ed Sheeran's *'Thinking Out Loud'*, I challenged the children to get a copy of the lyrics to their favourite pop song and up-level the grammar as their homework task. Children returned to school talking of Ellie Goulding's double negative and Adele's wrong subject–verb agreement!

As well as correcting the spelling, punctuation and grammar, in order to represent the song in standard English, children can colour-code the lyrics, identifying as much of the National Curriculum's Grammar Appendix as they can. Suddenly, expanded noun phrases, subordinating conjunctions and adverbial phrases become a lot of fun!

I spy

'I spy with my little eye . . .'

This traditional favourite is a great game to play at home, with lots of variations to support learning. It can literally be played anywhere, and is great for long car journeys!

Provide parents with a list of possible ways to play 'I spy' that they can easily dip into when they are out and about with their children. The great thing about 'I spy' is that it can be played at any age and can support different aspects of learning.

Suggested ways of playing:

I spy with my little eye . . .

- something beginning with (letter name)
- something beginning with (initial sound) – *for example, 'sh' for shoe, rather than the letter 's'*
- something ending in (letter name)
- something with (number of letters) – *this is useful as a way of practising spelling too*
- something rhyming with (rhyming word) – *for example, 'whale', to rhyme with 'snail'*
- something the colour (name the colour) – *this is particularly useful for very young children still learning colours, but you can get creative with older children by looking at examples of colours on paint strips, like fuchsia or mocha brown!*
- something (shape) – *this is useful when learning 2D and 3D shape names; you would be surprised at the variety of shapes around!*
- something used for . . . *eating, playing with, writing, washing.*

Teaching tip

It is worth providing parents with a list of games/activities that can be played as homework and referred to throughout the year, so as not to be forgotten. Displaying these on your class webpage is also handy for when – I mean, if – the paper copy goes missing!

Bonus idea ★

Ask children to share any of their own variations of the game – these can then be added to the class webpage.

Off by heart

'If you can learn a pop song by heart, you can learn a poem!'

The English Primary National Curriculum states that children should read, perform and learn poetry by heart. Learning poetry provides children with a powerful language bank as well as developing memory skills and improving reading. It is said that young children who know a bank of nursery rhymes by heart from a young age will be amongst the best readers at the age of eight.

Taking it further

Organise a Poetry Slam within your class, or across the school or year group. Invite children to recite and perform a poem of their choice, or an original one written by themselves. Poetry Slams coincide well with National Poetry Day, which takes place during the autumn term. See nationalpoetryday.co.uk for dates each year (as well as a wealth of poetry resources!).

Children will have preferred methods of learning poetry, and will not always take the same amount of time to confidently learn it by heart, so it is an ideal homework task. I usually like to set one poem per half term to be learnt by heart. This can be the same poem set for the whole class or, alternatively, you can set the children the challenge of finding and reciting their own.

The website www.poetrybyheart.org.uk contains an anthology of poems that can be learnt by heart, while the BBC's Poetry by Heart website contains clips of poems being read. These are great, as they really model the 'performance' element of poetry. Sharing YouTube clips of poetry performers such as Brian Moses, Michael Rosen and Benjamin Zephaniah (in class or via the class Padlet (see Idea 73 for more information on using Padlet), to be accessed at home) gives children the chance to see well-known poems being performed by their poets. The clips are definitely worth the children viewing before being expected to perform themselves, and they are also great fun to watch!

Mnemonics

'Big Elephants Can Always Understand Small Elephants.'

Many schools set a weekly list of spellings to be learnt, and it's worth sharing strategies with parents to enable them to support their children in learning and remembering tricky spellings.

A spelling mnemonic is a strategy that people use to aid their memories when it comes to those tricky words that often don't follow regular spelling patterns. Over the years, I have shared some well-known spelling mnemonics with children, although I often find they remember them more when they have devised their own.

Mnemonics can take different forms. They could be songs – the alphabet song, for example, is a great way of learning and remembering the letters of the alphabet. If you have read Roald Dahl's *Matilda*, you will be familiar with how Miss Honey teaches the word 'difficulty' by turning it into a song. Sentences or phrases, like 'There's a rat in sep*arat*e', or short rhymes – 'I before E except after C, when the sound is "ee"' – are also effective. Turning each letter of a word into a word from a sentence, as in the quote above, which spells 'because', or 'o u lucky duck' for c*ould*, sh*ould* and w*ould*, is another form of using a mnemonic to aid memory.

Teaching tip

Ensure the children are familiar with the idea of mnemonics before setting it as homework. Share some well-known examples and allow children to come up with their own. Send home a list of tricky words, or longer words needed for a new topic, and ask the children to create their own mnemonics to help them remember.

MATHS

Part 3

Shopping lists

'This really helped her to understand the concept of budgeting!'

I first started doing this with my daughter as a result of playing a board game called 'Shopping Lists', where the players compete to fill their trolleys with the required items. Writing out shopping lists can benefit English and maths skills, as well as develop a fundamental life skill!

Provide the children with a shopping list for a specific purpose. This could be a list of cooking ingredients or a list of things needed for a residential trip. Of course, the children won't need to actually buy these things, but must find out where the items can be bought from and how much they cost. Providing a budget for the children to keep to will add a challenge.

Younger children could be given a virtual £5 note and asked to find three different things that can be bought. Can they spend exactly £5? If not, how much change would they have left over? This can link nicely to themes as well: three items to take on holiday; three pieces of fruit; three Christmas presents; and so on.

Linking the task to something real gives purpose to the homework and gives a valuable insight into costs and budgeting. Of course, there is always opportunity to be more creative. During the Rio Olympics, a class of ten- and eleven-year-olds were asked to plan a trip to Brazil and three events they would like to see. This involved finding flights, hotels, tickets and so on. With no budget restrictions, these children enjoyed planning a rather luxurious trip!

Teaching an old dog

'If you can't explain it simply, you don't understand it well enough.'
Albert Einstein

In class, I know how well a child understands something when they are able to explain it back to me. Asking children to explain why something is true or false, for example, can be a good way of doing this. This homework task asks children to teach a concept to someone at home.

As teachers, we will all have heard parents explain how it was taught differently in their day. In fact, lots of what I teach I learnt differently in my day! So, for example, with so many calculation methods taught across the primary years, giving children opportunities to explain them and teach them to others will help to consolidate their understanding.

This homework idea works particularly well with maths. Concepts such as calculating using number lines, the grid method, and long multiplication and division are all understood better if the child is able to explain it to somebody else. It also gives parents an insight into the methods being taught.

Children can explain a method to a grown-up at home, providing examples and setting questions or tasks for their grown-up to complete. The 'student' can then evaluate the 'teacher'!

Teaching tip

Provide key vocabulary linked with the concept being taught. Ask children to explain the vocabulary and use it in their 'teaching'. Having the time to talk through methods and give reasons to support calculations will help to embed the learning further.

Taking it further . . .

Provide a bank of true and false statements, along with the keyword, 'because'. The statement might include something like $5 \times 6 = 5 + 6$. The pupils' challenge is to explain why the statement is false to somebody who really has no clue!

Recall

'Arithmetic is being able to count up to twenty without taking off your shoes.' Mickey Mouse

Providing a bank of quick-fire recall games that can be played at home throughout the year is a useful resource for parents in supporting their children.

Teaching tip

It is worth providing parents with a list of useful games to play at home at the start of the school year. These can be referred to in weekly homework, and a copy shared on the school website or stuck inside a homework book.

The importance of knowing number bonds and times tables facts cannot be stressed enough. So many mathematical concepts – and, in fact, day-to-day life – require a good basic understanding of number. Regular practice at school and at home can make all the difference.

- **Rock, paper, scissors**
  I regularly play this with my own children. It works as a fun lesson starter but can easily be played at home with families. The game works like the usual rock, paper, scissors, but each player instead chooses a different number of fingers to hold up. The first person to call out the total number of fingers (or, if two players, the numbers on each hand multiplied together) scores a point.
- **Fizz buzz**
  This classic game is an easy to play at home and great for learning tables. Choose a multiplication table to focus on. Count up from one, taking it in turns, then say 'fizz' when you come across a multiple of your chosen number (e.g. 5-1, 2, 3, 4, fizz, 6, 7, 8, 9, fizz). Then add another multiple, e.g. 3, for which you say 'buzz'. (1, 2, buzz, 4, fizz, buzz, 7, 8, buzz, fizz, 11, buzz, 13, 14, fizzbuzz!)
- **What's my number?**
  This is a great game for practising maths vocabulary being taught in class. Send home a list of words (odd, even, multiple, factor, square number, prime number, etc.) and ask

Taking it further

Include board games as part of the children's homework. Reading the dice, counting the number of squares forwards or backwards, working with money and following instructions are all beneficial to a child's general maths skills.

children to work with someone to guess their number. Choose a number between 1 and 100 (smaller or larger numbers depending on age) for the opposing player to work out using no more than ten questions. This can also work with 'shape' work, using vocabulary such as *angles, faces, sides, vertices, etc.*

- **Bingo!**
  Another great lesson starter that can easily be played at home. List six numbers between 1 and 144. The parent calls out multiplication questions for the child to try to find the answers to. This can easily be adapted for addition/subtraction/division as well.

- **Loose change**
  Ask children to work out how much loose change is their parent's purse or wallet. What payments could you make exactly? So a 50p, a 20p, three 5ps and a 2p equals 87p. What other exact amounts could be made using some of the coins? How much is needed to round to the next pound?

- **One-minute maths**
  A daily minute of arithmetic questions can dramatically speed up recall, and a slip of paper provided with quick-fire questions on the four calculations are easy to put together.

- **What is the question?**
  Provide a number for the children to investigate. How many ways/calculation methods can the children use to reach this number?

- **Memory**
  A pack of playing cards can have many uses. For learning number bonds, keep the cards from Aces to 10s and remove the Jacks, Queens and Kings. Turn each card upside down. Each player takes it in turns to pick two cards, trying to find a pair that makes 10. When a pair is found, that player keeps those cards. Players need to remember where each card is placed, rather than relying on luck!

Regular games at home don't require weekly marking. A short comment from the parent can let you know of any issues.

Number hunt

'There are numbers everywhere.'

Going on a number hunt helps children see that numbers really are everywhere and are used for a variety of purposes. Lots can be done with the numbers we see in our day-to-day lives.

Think of all the places we come across numbers. House numbers, road signs, food packaging, clocks, phones, car number plates, bank statements . . . the list goes on.

- **Recognising numbers**
  Children list the numbers they can find in and around their homes. They can record these numbers and list them in order.
- **Hunting for numbers**
  Make it more challenging by asking children to find numbers that measure weight, capacity, distance or time; numbers used in addresses or phone numbers; prime numbers; decimal numbers; multiples of nine and so on. The possibilities are endless.
- **Exploring the numbers**
  Listing the numbers in order is useful practice, and numbers like car mileage and telephone numbers add to the challenge. Practise rounding to the nearest 10, 100 or 1000. Finding the difference between the highest and lowest numbers also supports calculation strategies.

Bonus idea ★

Suggest the children choose how they record the numbers they find. This could be in a table, a drawing or even by photographing the numbers.

Timetabling

'I spend a lot of time on my computer!'

Maths tests always involve time problems. Working out how long it takes a bus to get from one town to another is a classic example often found in tests. Reading timetables is an essential skill, and this homework task provides a fun starting point.

Creating a weekend timetable can be very insightful, particularly as an adult! For children working on time problems in school, a weekend timetable provides a purposeful and personal homework challenge.

Over the course of the two days, children should record the times they start and finish particular activities. This can be recorded along a chronological timeline, in a more traditional timetable format, or listed by activity.

Once the children have recorded their weekend activities on their timetable, they can use the information to think about 'time'. How long did they spend sleeping, playing, eating, attending a club? Do they need to change any part of their lifestyle?

This can be adapted for younger children by asking them to draw clocks showing the different times they do different activities and reflect on the range of activities they do.

Teaching tip

The children's timetables, once complete, can be represented in different graphs. Pie charts and bar graphs can show the proportion of time spent doing different activities.

Taking it further

Use a local bus or train timetable for children to write their own questions. These questions can provide a great paired warm-up when back in school.

Measure

'I measured dinosaur bones.'

Applying maths to real-life contexts will help to embed children's understanding. This homework tasks looks at different ways of measuring around the home, and can be linked to topic work too.

Taking it further

Ask the children to measure one step in centimetres. How many steps would they need to take to walk 100 metres or 1 kilometre? Children with a pedometer could find out whether their calculations were accurate!

My five-year-old spent hours one afternoon happily measuring items around the house with a 30cm ruler. Who knew measuring could be so much fun? Equipped with a ruler or tape measure, this is a simple task to complete and record. If the children are familiar with language such as *longer than* and *shorter than*, this can be applied when discussing the measurements found.

During a history topic on Romans one year, I discovered that they measured distances using their feet. Ask your children to measure the length of their bedrooms, or other rooms around the house, by placing one foot in front of the other and counting how many feet it takes to walk across. Is the distance the same as when their parents measure the room? Can they explain why the measurement might be different?

Older children can have a go at measuring the perimeter and area of their bedrooms after becoming familiar with methods of finding each at school.

As well as measuring length, ask children to compare the weights of different household objects, either by holding items in each hand and deciding which is heavier and which is lighter, or using weighing scales. Another option is to look at capacity. Ask the children to look at food labels and compare measurements for weight and capacity. What are the different units of measurement?

Bonus idea ★

What is the most interesting object a child can find to measure? Compare findings when back in school.

Counting clocks

'We have a clock on our microwave!'

Teaching children to tell the time is always a tricky task. There are those children who will have learnt at home and those who will struggle to get it for a while. But, like riding a bike, once it's learnt, it's learnt! Because telling the time is something we do daily, there are plenty of opportunities to get children involved, in and out of school.

Once children are familiar with recognising analogue and digital clocks, ask them to literally count all of the clocks they can find at home. This might include anything from traditional wall-mounted analogue clocks and digital bedside table alarm clocks to the clocks on a mobile phone home screen or on the kitchen oven. One child I once taught even noted down the sundial in his grandparents' garden.

Ask the children to draw at least three of the clocks. What is the time on each clock? What do the different numbers mean? How long until the next hour? Can they identify 12-hour and 24-hour clocks?

Encourage parents to regularly ask the children what the time is. This can also include asking them how long until lunchtime, bedtime and so on. Ask children to note down the times they do specific activities, like eating breakfast, leaving for school or going to football club. This will help children to become immersed in telling the time and understand where different times fall in the 'whole day'.

Taking it further

Older children can write their own time problems based on the times of the clocks they find. For example: *When I sat down for breakfast, the kitchen clock was at 7:25 am. Five hours and 15 minutes passed before I sat down again for lunch. What time did I have lunch?*

Telephone keypad

'For some reason, using the numbers from a mobile phone made it more fun for the children.'

Recognising and ordering two- or three-digit numbers is an essential element of maths teaching in primary. Rather than sending home a worksheet of numbers to put into order, ask the children to find their own with the help of a mobile phone. Engagement levels will go up immediately!

Taking it further

Ask the children to look at mobile phone numbers. If these were real numbers, whose number is the highest? By how much? What number do they get if the phone numbers are added together?

Ask the children to borrow a mobile phone, and use the keypad. They should list a set number of two or three digit numbers, and then write these out in words. For example, 257 is two hundred and fifty-seven. As well as this, ask the children to list the numbers in order from smallest to largest.

Older children can create their own addition and subtraction calculations, finding the largest and smallest numbers that can be made. These calculations can be displayed similarly to the methods being used at school, so number lines or column method could be specified.

Other suggestions could involve finding the highest or lowest 3 digit number going from left to right, top to bottom, or even diagonally. What is the total when you add all of the numbers together?

The great thing about mobile phones is that they often come with a calculator, which children can use to check their calculations afterwards!

Longer or shorter?

'A really useful way of practising vocabulary beyond the classroom and in everyday conversation.'

The language we use to describe everyday items often involves the size of the object: 'My slice of cake is smaller than yours.' Encouraging conversation that refers to the size of objects can help to embed understanding of key measurement vocabulary.

Setting measurement homework can reinforce language taught in the classroom linked with height, weight and capacity, as well as link to learning of comparatives and superlatives (and their relevant suffixes).

Ask the children to list their family members in order of height, discussing the language of tallest, shortest and who is taller or shorter. An extension could be to measure their exact heights and find the differences.

Everyday objects that can be compared include reading books, food jars, fruit and — a real winner — the children's toys. Ask the children to feel the weight of different objects to decide which is heavier and lighter before actually weighing anything.

Provide the children with a vocabulary bank to be referred to while recording the sizes. This will also help parents to model the correct vocabulary.

Taking it further

Ask the children to find something that measures approximately 1 metre then list it against items that are longer and shorter. This will help children to visualise what 1 metre actually looks like.

Number line

'How much is a million?'

Children often learn to count before they understand what each number actually means. Counting individual objects is a skill in itself, which usually comes after being able to recall numbers 1–10. Early Years teachers will be familiar with children rolling off numbers, but whizzing ahead when it comes to counting items, resulting in the wrong total. Practising 'counting' and identifying different numbers in real life helps to embed a bit of understanding as to what these numbers actually mean!

Teaching tip

It is worth sharing with parents how everyday activities like counting items can really support learning in school. If this becomes a regular activity at home, it can only benefit the learning in the classroom.

Taking it further

Children can build on this back in school by finding and photographing certain quantities of pencils, Lego pieces, beanbags and so on.

The book *How Much is a Million?* by David M. Schwartz has always been a favourite of mine, and one I love to share with children. Larger numbers like one million are challenging for children to visualise and this book helps to put it into perspective. If you haven't read it with children yet, prepare to see jaws drop!

Even with much smaller numbers, it can take a while for children to recognise, for example, what '3' actually means. Provide the children with a number line – the length will depend on the age/ability of your students. Younger children learning numbers 1–10 can find an example of each number as part of their homework. This might include: one brother, two dolls, three pictures on the kitchen wall, four wheels on the car, 5 o'clock dinner time, six oranges and so on.

Older children, who need to be able to order larger numbers, could find populations of cities or countries you are studying and arrange them from smallest to largest.

SCIENCE

Part 4

Doctor, doctor

'A fun way to learn the different body parts.'

Variations of this game can be played to support the learning of different body parts and organs to suit different year groups.

Taking it further

This activity can also support learning in another language. Write the labels in a language being studied at school and play in the same way.

Ask the children to list different body parts on post-it notes. They should practise identifying the parts of the body by labelling a parent (or other willing patient!) with the correct post-its. For younger children, the labels might include head, back, arm, hand, leg and foot, and with older children, they could include brain, heart, lungs, biceps and so on.

A popular variation is for the adult to feign illness of a particular body part. The child can cure the ailment by placing the correct post-it onto the correct body part. This activity supports the reading and writing of key vocabulary, as well as identification of the main body parts. It works particularly well with younger children, as well as those learning English as an additional language.

Bonus idea ★

While identifying the different body parts, discuss what their purpose is. Do some body parts have more than one purpose?

Children can also consider and list who it is safe to take medicine from when they are feeling unwell. This can link well with older pupils learning about different types of drugs, and safety taking medication.

States of matter

'A great way of seeing science in daily life.'

Primary pupils are taught to recognise three states of matter (solids, liquids and gases). Encouraging them to identify these states in daily life, beyond a classroom experiment, adds purpose to the learning and a sense of 'realness'.

If homework is to be effective, it needs to support the learning taking place in the classroom and, ideally, be an opportunity to practise and apply knowledge and skills developed in school. Children love practical science experiments, and a favourite topic of mine is looking at materials and how they change. An obvious starting point is for children to be able to recognise different states of matter (and if you don't mention plasma, I'm sure a child will!).

Once children are confident in their understanding of solids, liquids and gases, including the properties of each, send them on a 'states of matter' hunt as their homework task. This can easily be organised in three boxes or columns, with examples of each recorded. Some examples to get them started could include: Lego and a cereal bowl, bath water and washing-up liquid, or steam from the kettle and gas from the cooker.

As well as within the home, what examples of each state can be identified outside? A slide, puddles and the smell of fish and chips can all be added to the list.

Teaching tip

Ensuring the children are confident with the concepts of the different states of matter and providing a few examples will make the homework a smoother ride, for the children and their parents!

Taking it further

When thinking about the changes to a state of matter, ask the children to identify those from their lists that can change and be placed into a different column as a result. For example, the steam from the kettle will condense and return to a liquid form. A puddle will evaporate and turn in to a gas.

What is it made from?

'This really helped the children to think about the purpose of using different materials.'

Different materials are all around us and are chosen to fit the purpose. In science lessons, children have opportunities to identify different materials and group them on the basis of their properties, including their 'hardness, solubility, transparency, conductivity and response to magnets' (English National Curriculum). It is a worthwhile activity to ask children to explore everyday items at home, identifying the materials used and the reasons why.

Taking it further

Set a challenge to design something for a specific purpose. This could be a camping cup, an umbrella or a new school PE kit. The children must choose the materials carefully and be able to explain why they are fit for purpose.

This is another homework activity that allows children to practise using the key vocabulary learnt in school. Provide each child with a list of terminology (I also send these home over a term to be included in spelling practice) to be used as part of the homework. Ask the children to list a range of everyday items they use, or which are used by family members, as well as the materials used to make the items, and reasons why they are a suitable choice.

Give some examples that can be referred to and used as a guide for when the children are finding their own. This could include a saucepan made from metal, as it conducts heat and won't melt, with a plastic handle to insulate the heat. A simple way to organise the homework would be to have four columns for the item, material, property and purpose.

Bonus idea ★

Ask the children to create a 'feely' book for a toddler, collecting different materials that would provide a safe sensory experience.

Item	Material	Property	Purpose
Window	Glass	Transparent	See-through
		Waterproof	Keeps the rain out
		Double-glazed	Insulates the heat

It's alive

'It does all of Mrs Nerg!'

I am sure there are many acronyms used to recall the seven life processes. Mrs Nerg has always been a favourite of mine, though I have seen her friend, Mrs Gren, appear in some classrooms! Living things are all around us, and it is important for children to see this beyond a science worksheet or a plant.

Once the children have become familiar with the seven life processes (movement, respiration, sensitivity, nutrition, excretion, respiration and growth), challenge them to make a list of 'living things' in and around their homes. This can include family members, pets and plants.

To provide challenge, the children can group the living things, applying terminology being used in the classroom. It is useful to provide a word bank that the children can refer to. Vocabulary might include: vertebrates, invertebrates, mammals, reptiles, minibeasts, insects, fish, amphibians and so on. Children can choose how they present their findings, although they will need to consider the terminology carefully, as many living things can be labelled as more than one thing, e.g. vertebrate and fish.

Additionally, children can choose three of their 'living things' and find out/label how they exercise the seven different life processes.

Taking it further

Back in school (or as an additional homework challenge if the children feel confident enough), get the children to make a classification key based on approximately six to eight of the living things they spotted in and around their homes.

May the force be with you!

'A great opportunity to recognise forces in action beyond the classroom worksheet'.

Understanding 'forces in action' allows children to answer a lot of their own questions, like 'What makes a boat float?' or 'How do aeroplanes fly?' Identifying forces in action in the world around them helps children to make a bit more sense of the world and allows you, as the teacher, to identify any misconceptions.

Taking it further

Ask the children to design their own parachute or snow mobile, thinking carefully about the materials chosen (links well with Idea 33) and the forces in action. Create a blueprint to be shared back in class.

Once the children are familiar with different forces in the classroom, set them the challenge of finding different examples of each force in and around their homes. The task can be adapted to suit your pupils, perhaps focusing on one or two particular forces. Younger children might just look for examples of push and pull forces, whereas the older children could be encouraged to identify friction, air resistance and so on. A challenge like this encourages children to explore everyday objects, as well as look deeper at technology and nature around them.

Ask the children to draw examples of forces in action, including labels and arrows to show the direction of each force. It is useful to provide examples of what the children could include – for instance, the forces in action of a child on a swing, a child swimming, a child riding a bike, using scissors, a bird flying and so on. This will give the children (and parents) an idea of what to look out for.

Phases of the moon

'An opportunity to make the learning real!'

It is easy to talk about the phases of the moon in class, and there is a plethora of video clips and apps that demonstrate each phase, but there's nothing quite like looking up to the sky with the naked eye and seeing for yourself how it changes shape and position in the sky across the month.

Either provide the children with a template containing 28 blank circles, or invite them to choose their own method of recording the moon each night. Ask the children to check every evening and draw, photograph or find another means of showing the shape and the date.

Of course, should a cloudy evening occur, invite the children to use the Internet to research the moon phase and add the information to their own findings. Alternatively, they can leave a blank moon, and carry on the following evening. Can they estimate what the visible shape of the moon was on that cloudy evening?

It is important to ensure that the children understand that the shape of the moon is not actually changing, but only the part of the moon that is visible to us.

Teaching tip

A favourite nowadays is to use Oreo biscuits, by removing one side of biscuit and then cutting away the cream inside to represent the shape of the moon. Obviously a full moon wouldn't require any cream tampering! Pinterest is full of pictures of this example in practice, and I am yet to meet a child who doesn't love this way of recording each phase – after all, what is one to do with the biscuit and cream that's been taken away?

Taking it further

As part of the homework, or back in class, ask the children to create a fact-file explaining the phases of the moon. This will help to demonstrate understanding and allow you to pick up on any misconceptions.

Minibeast hunt

'A perfect outdoor activity to support learning in science.'

Primary curriculums require children to learn about animals and their habitats, including micro-habitats. This fun homework task gets children and their families outdoors and supports the learning back in the classroom.

Taking it further

Get your school eco club to create minibeast hotels for the school grounds. Not only are you helping your local environment, but you are also creating a fantastic resource for the children in school. Ask children to design a hotel as homework before making it at school.

Explore the meaning of 'habitats', including how animals are suited to their own habitats and how these can change throughout the year. Once the children are familiar with this, set a minibeast hunt homework task. It is worth giving at least a week to complete this, as it will require families having the time to get outside and hunt for the minibeasts.

Organisations like The Woodland Trust have some amazing resources on their websites. Use these to support the children with their hunt. Identification sheets and recording tables will be useful, as well as tips on where to look!

You might suggest the children take an empty yoghurt pot to allow them to collect a minibeast and study it further. Remember to stress the importance of being careful and putting the minibeast back as soon as possible.

Another option is for children to create their own minibeast hotels using natural materials and old plant pots. Once the hotel has been made and left, the children can visit it regularly to see its guests! Search for 'minibeast hotel' on the Internet to see examples and instructions that can be shared with the children.

Who discovered what?

'A useful homework task to run alongside all science topics.'

Primary science teaching often involves the children finding out about scientists, naturalists and even animal behaviourists. Setting homework to find out about such people not only frees up some time in the classroom, but also supports research, presentation skills and, importantly, a further understanding of the science topic being studied.

One option is to set the children an open-ended research project where they can choose a scientist or you ask them to find out about one in particular. Software like Google Classroom will allow the children to collaborate on such projects and prepare a presentation together. Padlet is also useful here (see Idea 73 for more information on Padlet), as children can share any information or links to relevant sites.

Children could create a fact-file about the scientist's life, discoveries and what effect these have had on the world. Collated, these can make an effective display or non-fiction resource, as well as contribute to the child's overall work produced during the topic.

I recently discovered the BP Educational Service website, which includes resources that can be shared with children in their research. This is definitely worth a visit, either to share as homework or to use in the classroom.

Back in school, encourage children to share their research. This can be done on class tables or as a more formal presentation to the class, which can also support your speaking and listening assessments.

Teaching tip

It is worth ensuring you suggest a range of male and female scientists to be researched, as many children still visualise all scientists looking like Albert Einstein!

Bonus idea ★

Ask the children to create a short quiz. This could be via software like Kahoot or Plickers, or by using a more traditional means (jotting down the answer!).

Keeping healthy

'The mini-project supported so much learning in science and PSHE.'

Along with encouraging children to eat their '5 a day', homework that focuses on the importance of exercise and general healthy living can have a positive impact back in the classroom.

Ask children to list different ways they exercise in and out of school, as well as sporting activities that they know other people do. As part of the homework, ask the children to choose a simple exercise, like running, skipping, hopping or jumping and note down how they feel after completing the exercise for three minutes. Their ideas are likely to include *'my breathing was quicker'* and *'I felt warmer'*. After sharing these observations back in the classroom, explore what happens during exercise and why it is good for us.

During a general 'keeping healthy' theme, children can consider other aspects that keep us fighting fit. Expected outcomes will vary depending on the age of the children you teach. As a mini project, ask the children to create information for a local health centre, detailing the different ways to look after themselves. Ideas might include:

- medicines and legal/illegal drugs
- sun safety and the importance of sunscreen
- looking after our teeth and making regular dental appointments
- the importance of regular exercise
- healthy eating and drinking plenty of fluids
- keeping clean/washing our hands
- getting enough sleep/how sleep affects our behaviour.

Bonus idea ★

Ask the children to make a personal pledge to keep healthy, stating how they will strive to achieve this. It might include *going to bed on time, eating a portion of vegetables with my meal* or *walking to and from school as much as possible*.

Don't forget your 5 a day

'It encouraged children to think of creative ways to get their fruit and veg in.'

Healthy eating is always on the agenda in schools — healthy schools weeks, objectives in science and PSHE, and even on the School Improvement Plan for some. Asking children to design their own healthy menus, and prepare the food as well, is a great way to get children thinking about their own diets and learning skills in the kitchen.

Spend time with the children discussing what is meant by a healthy and balanced diet. This can be linked to learning in science around the food pyramid or as part of a whole-school agenda to promote healthier eating. At home, ask the children to design a healthy two-course meal that could appear on the school lunch menu.

The menu can be planned and designed in a format that would attract diners to choose the food. Encourage the children to prepare the meal (with help) at home and evaluate it against a range of criteria. They might consider the cost, preparation time, nutritional values, appearance and, of course, the taste!

Ask the children to share their menus back in school and vote for those that sound most appetising as well as healthy. Which menus most effectively help the children to take in their 5 a day?

Taking it further

As well as the menu, link the learning to your maths and English work by asking the children to write out the recipes, including the features of instructional texts. Children could include measurements and consider the proportions needed for different numbers of people.

TOPICS

Part 5

Takeaway homework

'The children love the freedom of choice that the takeaway menu offers.'

I first came across 'takeaway homework' on Twitter through Ross Morrison McGill (@TeacherToolkit) and it wasn't long before we were rolling it out across our primary school. And what a success it has been! Although perhaps not for every school, we have found that providing a choice of creative tasks has engaged pupils and produced fabulous outcomes.

For those of you unfamiliar with the term 'takeaway homework', let me explain. Children are provided with a homework menu that contains a list of homework choices. These usually include starters, mains and desserts, and I ask the children to choose at least one from each section, as you might from a restaurant menu. The homework choices are linked with the current topic, although may cover a range of subjects or skills. A quick Google search will show a wealth of examples that kind teachers from around the globe have shared.

In a bid to make our takeaway homework 'primary-friendly', each menu is set around the class's current theme or topic. Through a creative curriculum, our topics change each half term or term, and the choice of takeaway task is based on deepening knowledge and understanding of that specific topic. The children absolutely love being able to choose from their menu.

The first takeaway menu I put together was for my class of ten- and eleven-year-olds on the theme of disasters. Options ranged from making an A–Z list of natural disasters, to designing a warning device, to building an exploding volcano, to sketching a bush-fire scene.

We end each topic with an open exhibition where each child is able to display their takeaway homework to visiting classes and parents.

Top tips for primary takeaway homework:

- Provide at least 12 tasks to choose from.
- Organise the tasks into three sections (starter, main, dessert), depending on complexity, and ask the children to complete at least one of each.
- Include activities that can link to learning in a range of subject areas.
- Give each child a copy of the menu, but also keep a copy on the classroom door or the class page of the school website for those who will always manage to lose their own copy!
- Post a copy on the class Padlet (see Idea 73 for using Padlet) and invite children to share ideas.
- Provide an hour or so, every now and again, to offer in-class support or access to resources that some pupils might struggle to get their hands on at home. The app iMovie is a fantastic resource but few children have it at home.
- Hold an exhibition at the end for children and parents to visit. Leave post-it notes near each child's personal exhibition for the visitors to give feedback. (This also helps out with your own feedback!)

Bonus idea ★

Leave a couple of blank takeaway options to allow children to add their own ideas.

Top Trumps

'A fun and engaging way to learn key information.'

Top Trumps cards are a popular game among children, as any teachers who have had to confiscate them during a lesson will testify to! They are actually a useful way of learning information in many curriculum areas and children love making their own, too.

Teaching tip

Go through methods of researching information before setting the homework. Model using websites and reference books to source the key information required.

I often give a 'Top Trumps' option on my Takeaway homework (see Idea 41 for more information on Takeaway homework) menu, as they are fun to make and can contain important information linked to your current topic. For example, in a class learning about the Tudors, ask the children to create their own Top Trumps cards (a range of templates are available online) giving information about Tudor monarchs. This could include the number of years they reigned, their age when crowned, the number of marriages and the children they had.

It is also a great way to learn about different minibeasts, as children can research and list the number of legs, wings, shells and stings, for example.

Maths cards can have times tables or other calculations given so that the player needs to work them out in order to find the number. For example, Superman's power might be 6x7, as opposed to Batman's, at 4x9.

The cards, once made, can be played at home with families or brought back into school to be shared with friends.

Inventors

'Faction is so useful when the focus is on the writing.'

I often find one of the biggest challenges children face when writing non-fiction texts is the worry that the factual content won't be accurate. Whilst children are still in the process of learning a text-type, allow them to be creative with the factual content.

I first heard the term 'faction' mentioned by Alan Peat, and it is one I refer to often. Homework time is a great opportunity for children to get creative with content, share ideas with family, and then return to school ready to write.

Before the children are expected to apply the features of a non-fiction text to other curriculum areas, practise this writing using 'faction'. Ask the children to plan something at home that supports the writing genre. This could be a new minibeast or planet or machine, which they can use as the content.

Younger children who design their own minibeasts can write a report when back at school, providing information on its appearance, diet, habitat and so on. Older children learning about pulleys, levers and springs can design a new machine and return to school able to explain how it works, using the text features taught in school.

Children love being able to use faction in their writing, and the practice of writing in a particular text-type can lead to improved writing when applying it to the curriculum.

> **Bonus idea** ★
>
> Each November is non-fiction month. Collect exemplary pieces of non-fiction writing and create a school encyclopaedia that can be added to the library.

Time capsule

'What would you like the future children of our school to know about today?'

Timelines are super for developing children's chronological understanding, and a great way of demonstrating where we are in relation to a range of historical periods.

Teaching tip

Create a time capsule representing a period of history you are studying before setting the homework. Discuss what the items tell us about that particular era. This will give the children a sense of audience and purpose when it comes to creating their own.

I always enjoy teaching lessons that involve discovering and exploring artefacts from a historical period we are learning about. Studying photographs, letters, newspaper clippings and even toys and items of clothing or household equipment leads to some fascinating thoughts, questions and discussions with the children. Comparing everyday items with what we use today allows us to see how society has evolved.

In preparation for burying a class or school time capsule, ask the children to think of things that represent 'today' that are likely to have changed in the next 100, 500 or 1000 years. After all, who knows when it might be discovered?

Some ideas might include:

- a popular children's book (or series)
- a popular toy (think of the latest craze!)
- maps of the local area and world – how might borders have changed in the future?
- a list of endangered species
- a leaflet for a local attraction
- a photograph of the local high street
- a textbook or copy of some children's work

Bonus idea

To encourage children to be slightly creative about their choice (or choices), set up a competition where only six items (or one per class across the school) will be chosen for the capsule. Children can also be encouraged to bury their own!

The children can be as imaginative as they want to be but should be able to return to school able to explain why they have chosen these items and how they represent the current period of living.

Advertising campaign

'Perfect for bringing enterprise projects alive.'

Television and magazine adverts provide a wealth of stimuli in teaching, from SPaG and persuasive writing to advertisement campaigns for the latest design technology project.

Ask the children to find examples of adverts for homework. These can be sourced from newspapers, magazines, billboards, YouTube and, of course, television. Allow the children to choose how to record the adverts. They can identify the features they have explored in class, such as slogans, wordplay, hyperbole and so on, as well as explain what makes the advert successful (or not!).

Linking with SPaG, adverts are wonderful for looking at expanded noun phrases. The famous Marks and Spencer adverts, '*This is not just . . .*', work as a great example. Ask the children to find examples of expanded noun phrases and the 'head noun'. Adjectives, adverbs and other grammar terminology being learnt can also be part of the advert grammar hunt.

Link it with a design technology project – perhaps some cooking, or a product that has been sewn or built – where the children can also consider their intended 'buyers' and put together billboard adverts or flyers, giving information and persuading 'customers' to buy the product. If the children are able to visualise who their product is for, it helps not only in their advertising campaign, but also in the design and finish of the overall product.

Bonus idea ★

Young Enterprise projects are a great way of getting youngsters thinking about 'business'. The website https://www.young-enterprise.org.uk/ provides information and projects that can be run in school and that support curriculum learning brilliantly.

The museum

'It was a lovely way to follow up our trip to the museum.'

Off-site visits often provide learning opportunities that the classroom just can't replicate. For one, the Natural History Museum's Dippy the Diplodocus just wouldn't fit in a standard classroom (though I do hear he's going on tour)! But with many classrooms providing role-play and immersive environments, a DIY museum (created by the children) is a brilliant second!

Taking it further

Ask the children to create adverts and information leaflets for the museum, which can be copied and distributed on the day the museum opens.

Creating your own museum works well if it coincides with a real visit to a real museum. Explain to the children that the class is putting on an exhibition for the rest of the school, as well as for the children's families at the end of the term. The children's job is to provide an artefact that can be displayed, along with some information about it.

This can be set as part of a Takeaway homework project (see Idea 41 for information on Takeaway homework), or as a stand-alone activity, but is a useful way of supporting topic learning in the classroom.

Provide examples of what might be included, such as weapons, armour, jewellery, scrolls, paintings, bones, statues and so on. Mummified dolls or Viking family flags are the sort of thing you might see appearing in your museum!

The homework task requires the children to undertake some research in order to make their exhibit as accurate as possible. It also provides a welcome alternative to homework sheets and an opportunity to showcase children's artefacts within the school community.

How do people express their faiths?

'A simple research activity to support learning in RE.'

This task can be adapted to allow the children to research a religion of their choice or a specific religion, or to present information on their own faith.

One of the items on The British Values agenda is mutual respect for, and tolerance of, those with different faiths and beliefs. It is often a lack of understanding that breeds fear or prejudice, and so it is vitally important that children understand the beliefs and customs of people's faiths.

Devise a list of questions for children to research and answer based on a particular faith.

These might include:

- Where is the religion's place of origin?
- Who do people of this faith pray to/worship?
- Does the faith have a sacred text? What is it called?
- What do people of this faith believe?
- How is this faith similar/different to other faiths?
- What are the holy days of obligation?
- How do people of this faith express their beliefs?
- What is the symbol of this faith?

Invite children to share their research back in school, or display it in a communal area such as the school library.

Bonus idea ★

Trips to local places of worship or invitations to local people of different religious orders can greatly benefit the children's understanding. If research is conducted beforehand, it opens up opportunity for a deeper discussion.

Timeline

'The dinosaurs lived on earth much longer than they have been extinct!'

Children often have trouble visualising where their lives fit in history. Seeing exactly when the dinosaurs, Ancient Greeks or Tudors lived in comparison to now, or when significant events took place, like the Great Fire of London or World War II, can be a real eye-opener. This homework task encourages children to think about where we are now in relation to the past and what is yet to come.

At Durlston Country Park in Dorset, there is a walk you can take, which is set out as a timeline going right back to when the Earth began. The timeline zigzags around the woodland and leads you to the castle, starting over 4 billion years ago and leading you to the present day. On a recent school trip, the guide explained to the children that the final 4mm of the walk shows all of human life. Our jaws dropped!

Ask the children to draw out a timeline (you might want to send home large sheets of paper to help with this). On it, they must pinpoint where they are now, as well as when they were born, and choose three historical periods to mark on the timeline as well. If you are studying a particular period in history this can be specified. Maths skills will also be required, as children can draw their timeline to scale.

This activity helps with children's chronological understanding and where the present day fits amongst history. In addition, the children can plot and predict future events – what will the year be when they are 25 or 50? What will be happening in the world? What will they be doing?

Bonus idea ★

This activity is useful to link alongside positive and negative numbers in maths. Look at key dates from both BC and AD. Set challenges to find the number of years between different events.

Island getaway

'The project required children to apply skills from all areas of the curriculum.'

Basic geographical skills can be developed creatively in this activity, which tasks children with designing their own island. Compass bearings and directional language can be practised and links can be made across the curriculum.

This project can be adapted to suit any year group and can run for as long as required. Supply children with a large sheet of squared paper, which is to become the map of their very own island. Grid reference skills will need to be applied as well as compass directions, supporting learning in maths and geography.

Provide a list of requirements for the children to meet. This can include:

- places of interest/a key
- how people can get to the island (if it's possible)
- details of the inhabitants
- the history of the island
- the variety of coastlines
- a postcard
- an island flag
- a 3D model of the island.

Children will love the element of choice and it is wonderful to see the variety of islands that the children come up with. Ask the children to present their islands to the class or group and include some key facts and perhaps some hidden treasure somewhere, only to be found by following the clues provided.

Taking it further

This can work with a whole topic in school, too, bringing together learning from many curriculum areas.

Bonus idea ★

The project is great to run alongside a class book, such as the *Katie Morag* series by Mairi Hedderwick, and links well with Idea 14 Desert Island Discs. Opportunities for writing include postcards, messages in a bottle, adverts to visit the island, a non-chronological report and even a folklore tale or song.

Dream jars

'"We is in Dream Country," the BFG said. "This is where all dreams is beginning."' Roald Dahl, *The BFG*

Anyone who has read *The BFG* will be familiar with dream jars. London was filled with them during the summer of 2016, when they became quite the tourist attraction. Creating personal dream jars is a great way to support class work on *The BFG*, and also links well with PSHE work on dreams, and rights and responsibilities.

Part 1:

To start with, ask pupils to keep a dream diary, writing a label for each dream to be placed onto its jar. Websites like Pinterest have examples and templates of labels to save time. Can any of the dreams be mixed up to create new ones?

Back in school, children can share the dreams they had (if willing) and the labels they gave them. Discuss the difference between the dreams we have at night and the dreams we have that include our hopes, wishes and ambitions.

Part 2:

Ask the children to spend time at home thinking about their personal dreams. What goals do they hope to achieve? Give the children some ownership over how they present the homework. Some may want to complete a piece of creative writing on a jar template, whereas others may want to fill and decorate an old jam jar. Having a range of differently designed dream jars makes looking at the homework when it returns far more interesting for the teacher and the other children.

THE ARTS

Part 6

5 a day sketch

'Thank you for bringing some peace and balance into my life.'

During October half term 2015, I led the first #teacher5aday #sketch – an initiative to get teachers taking time out to notice and sketch. The above quote is from Nina Jackson, an education consultant, who hasn't stopped sketching as a result! Many of us are so busy in our day-to-day lives, including the children we teach, that it is important to find time for peace and balance. Sketching homework allows time for just that.

Art homework has been a huge success as part of the #student5aday initiative at my school, particularly sketching, as it requires very little in terms of resources. Personally, I don't mark the sketching homework, and it is up to the children whether they choose to share it. For me, the homework is an opportunity for the children to stop, sit and notice, as they take time to really study something as they sketch it.

The sketching activities can be linked to artwork in school. Sketch in the style of a known artist, or apply skills learnt. The initial #teacher5adaysketch suggestions can provide a good starting point for sketch activities at home.

- Sketch three things you keep in your school bag.
- Sketch a piece of food.
- Sketch your favourite piece of artwork.
- Sketch an object you use every day.
- Sketch a special person or place.
- Sketch a place you would like to visit.
- Sketch the cover of your favourite book.

An ongoing gallery of sketches can be displayed for the children who wish to share their artwork.

Artist study

'Every child is an artist.' Picasso

The English Primary National Curriculum states that pupils must learn about 'great artists' and their work. A mini project, focusing on a specific artist or an artist of the child's choice, can really support learning going on in school and free up some of the curriculum timetable.

There is a wealth of amazing artists and art pieces that can be studied over the course of primary school, and setting this as a mini project is a creative alternative to more traditional homework. It is worth each school having a long-term plan when it comes to art, so artist studies aren't repeated across year groups.

A common topic is pop art, and so someone like Andy Warhol would be the obvious artist to study. Mini project tasks could include:

- Research and list five facts about Warhol's life.
- Name five pieces of art by Warhol.
- Which is your favourite piece of art by Warhol? Why?
- How does the artwork make you feel?
- What questions would you ask the artist about this piece?
- Create your own version of this piece.
- Create another piece of art in the same style.

The homework can contribute to the ongoing artwork in class and can be shared as part of a communal display back in school.

Taking it further

Rather than studying a particular artist, choose a theme or event you are studying in another curriculum area. This works well with subjects like RE, where children can choose their own artwork linked with stories like Noah's Ark, or in geography when studying, for example, mountains or rivers. Children can research a variety of pieces of art and consider the artists' interpretations, as well as create their own pieces.

Turn up the volume

'Music is the medicine of the mind.' John A. Logan

Music plays a significant role in many of our lives. Certain songs will have the power to bring back memories, instil a sense of nostalgia, motivate us or make us weep! There is a huge range of possibilities for children's learning when it comes to homework that involves listening to their favourite tunes, as well as providing a bit of chill-out time.

Children will often be more motivated to get stuck into their homework when there is an element of choice. Ask the children to listen to the radio, or some saved music they have at home. Sitting or lying down and just *listening* to the music can be a way to unwind after a busy day.

If you want to suggest some activities to go alongside the 'listening', ask the children to choose one of their favourite songs. Listening to the lyrics can be a great way to support comprehension. What is the 'story' of the song? How does the singer feel? How do the instrumentals contribute to the overall mood of the song?

Ask the children to choose different songs for different purposes. What music would be appropriate for a birthday party, a wedding ceremony, a car journey or simply to relax to? Which songs have the power to evoke different emotions?

Bonus idea ★

Allow the children to bring in their own music to be played at the end of each term. This could be a prize for those who've completed homework tasks, or for the winning house or class table.

Outdoor art

'A lovely way to really explore nature.'

Creating art from nature is not only a fun and creative activity to do, but also allows children to really explore nature, as well as develop a range of art techniques. Many have also commented on how therapeutic it can be!

Autumn is often the perfect time to get outside and create art using nature, although it is worth exploring the outdoors through all seasons! Fallen leaves of varying colours, twigs and bark are just waiting to be explored.

Art homework ideas could include:

- leaf prints – paint leaves of different sizes and create repeating patterns
- collages – use sand, twigs and leaves to create collage scenes
- collect a variety of natural resources to fill a clear plastic bottle – these can be layered (sand, soil, pebbles, leaves, twigs, grass, daisies, petals, etc.)
- plan and create a miniature garden
- bark rubbings using wax or crayon
- imitate animal art in the style of David Klein.

Back in school, create an outdoor exhibition where the art can be displayed and shared with the rest of the school community.

Taking it further

Provide a scrapbook, or encourage children to start one, so they can produce art at home at their leisure.

Comic strips

'Comics are always a favourite in the reading corner so this homework was happily received.'

Graphic novels and comics are often a popular choice in the school library and are ideal for inspiring reading for pleasure. Asking the children to create their own comic strips is not only a brilliant art activity, but also a great way to hook children into reading.

Taking it further

Back in school, children can work in groups to create comic strips of scenes from the class book. Photograph freeze frames of key moments and use apps like Comic Life or Strip Designer to create the comic strip. This is a great way of getting drama into your lessons, and the production of a comic strip means it can be shared with an audience.

Study a range of graphic novels and comics in school. I often use them to support teaching of direct speech, where the speech bubbles are taken and written out as dialogue. The vast amount of totally brilliant graphic novels means there are too many to list here, but some favourites include Raymond Briggs' *Fungus the Bogeyman,* David Almond's *The Savage* and Bill Watterson's *Calvin and Hobbes* books.

For homework, ask the children to create their own comic strip, retelling a scene from their favourite, or current, reading book. It is definitely worthwhile looking at the art within graphic novels and comic strips before setting this homework. Discuss use of colour, the size and shape of the boxes and how facial expressions and background pictures can share a lot of the information.

Should your school library permit, allow the children to take home a comic strip or graphic novel that can be used as inspiration and bit of a 'how to' guide.

Collage portraits

'A creative activity that allows the children to present information about themselves in a different way.'

Collage activities are a favourite when learning about artists such as Pablo Picasso or Giuseppe Arcimboldo. One idea is for children to create collage portraits of themselves, showcasing some special facts they would like to share, too.

Look at examples of collages and have a go at imitating some famous ones in the classroom. Giuseppe Arcimboldo's artwork, which uses fruit to create portraits, is a classroom favourite, where pictures from supermarket leaflets can be used to make similar portraits.

As homework, ask the children to create a collage portrait. They can draw the outline of their heads, and then use drawings, photographs, texts or cut-outs to fill the portrait. The images and colours chosen should share some information about the children, such as family and friends, hobbies and interests, likes and dislikes.

This works brilliantly as a start-of-the-year homework activity as it can provide insightful information about the children, as well as contribute towards a cracking display featuring the entire class.

An alternative is for children to create collages of a particular book character or person from history, using materials and pictures that demonstrate their understanding of the character.

Teaching tip

Create a collage portrait of yourself, firstly as a model of what you expect, but also as a little insight into you beyond being the children's class teacher. Get Teaching Assistants involved too!

Bonus idea ★

Photograph the collages and upload to a movie software package. Add music and arrange the pictures to change every few seconds. Upload the montage to your class webpage, entitled, 'We are Class . . .'

Christmas cards

'A brilliant way to raise money for school.'

For those teachers looking to avoid any activity involving glitter (certainly not me!), this Christmas homework activity is ideal, plus it helps to raise funds for your school.

Teaching tip

Class-made crafts make magnificent displays during the Christmas period and any other festival celebrated throughout the year. Get them made as soon as is 'socially acceptable' so that you can maximise the time they are on the wall.

Bonus idea ★

Although this can free up class time (as well as raising money for school), I would also suggest getting the children to make a card in school, just for their immediate families, as an added surprise. It means that glitter lovers like me don't need to pack it away for good and, it has to be said, there's nothing quite like the hum of 'classroom elves' and festive tunes in the background.

As primary teachers, we are often wary of ensuring a fine balance at Christmas time between keeping the learning going (certainly my priority!) and embracing all things festive. Of course there are ways in which we can keep the teaching and learning high on the agenda disguised as a Christmas activity (festive maths and letter-writing to Santa Claus are definite favourites), but we need to be cautious that the final weeks of the autumn term don't become lost to Christmas films and never-ending craft-making. Apologies if I sound a little like Scrooge here.

One thing my school does is to ask the children to create a Christmas card at home. This is with the help of a company that provides templates, ideas and an order form! Once the card has been designed, it can be returned to school and multiple copies produced at a cost, if desired. The cards are returned with the designer's name (the child's) printed on the back, and they are perfect for families to send out to loved ones. What's more, the school receives a commission. Simply search online for 'school Christmas cards'.

If the Christmas card project is run by your PTA or art leader, it takes the pressure of paperwork and collecting cards away from the school office staff and class teachers.

Illuminated lettering

'Art homework can be a brilliant way to enhance learning in other subjects.'

There are so many opportunities to link your art objectives with other curriculum areas. Illuminated lettering is not only beautiful, but also links well with learning in subjects like history and religious education.

An illumination is an embellishment that enhances the written page. It is also one of the few homework pieces I remember from my own primary school days and has been popular with children I have taught.

Illuminated letters are great to set alongside history topics like the Egyptians, the Anglo-Saxons and the Vikings, as well as Medieval Britain. There are vast examples available of illuminated lettering and manuscripts online. The Lindisfarne Gospels is an illuminated manuscript gospel book – the pictures are an ideal resource to share when looking at illuminated artwork.

After sharing examples, ask the children to create their own illuminated letters as homework. This can be the initial of the child's name or you could give them a specific letter in order to create a display banner back in the classroom. They might consider a mythical creature, floral decoration or other drawings that represent the historical period being studied.

Setting the task as homework allows the children to spend as much time as they need on the task and develop a personalised letter. Art homework is also gratefully received, particularly by the older children, who occasionally feel bogged down with English and maths.

Bonus idea ★

Get the children to research the history of illuminated lettering and manuscripts.

Scrapbook

'A lovely project celebrating primary school.'

Creating a scrapbook can be done at any time, but for pupils to complete one during their final term at primary school makes it extra special. A collection of photos, captions, memories and even messages from others will make the scrapbook a treasured keepsake.

Upon leaving my first school, I was presented with a scrapbook containing photos, pictures and memories from the pupils and staff, and it really is something I will keep forever.

The scrapbook project will need to be spread over a half term at least, to allow pupils plenty of time to collect and arrange their materials. Some allocation of class time is also useful, with examples of scrapbook pages provided as a guide.

Many children choose a theme such as a sport, hobby or favourite subject. Allow the children to personalise the layout, choosing whether to arrange pages by year group or particular events.

Invite the children to share any pictures, memories or comments on the class Padlet so that they can be accessed and used by other children, too. Some favourites to include are:

- copies of photographs
- drawings or doodles
- journal entries or memory write-ups
- captions
- certificates
- messages from friends or teachers
- any copies of special school work from across the years
- a letter to themselves . . . what are their hopes and dreams? This is always interesting to read back on ten-plus years later.

Picture a story

'A great alternative to a traditional comprehension sheet.'

Children love the opportunity to draw. Even with older primary-aged children, if there is an opportunity to add a drawing to any writing, their eyes tend to light up. This homework task is all about drawing.

Provide children with a text, perhaps focusing on setting or character, and challenge them to draw it. A good example is the initial description of Mr Tumnus in *The Lion, the Witch and the Wardrobe,* or just the description of the Gruffalo, without any pictures to refer to. Children need to use their comprehension skills to piece together the character or the setting as best they can, perhaps using extracts from the text to label their pictures.

Another option is to create a comic strip (see Idea 55) showing the different sections of a short story, possibly in the format of a story mountain, or a picture to show a poem. *Hey, Diddle, Diddle* works brilliantly for this.

Alternatively, ask the children to choose their own scene from a favourite book, the current class book or a well-known poem, and draw a picture of how they visualise it. Create a display back in school (in the library, if possible, as this will open up your audience), where other children can try to work out which text the picture comes from.

Teaching tip

To flip things around, use the absolutely brilliant site www.onceuponapicture. co.uk. The webpage contains different images for each day to inspire writing. Provide children with a few to choose from to inspire their next piece of writing.

THE OUTDOORS

Part 7

Local study

'I've drawn the route I cycle to school.'

Before children start to study contrasting environments, it is important that they have a good grasp of their own locality. Map-reading and a sense of understanding of where we are in the world provides a base before moving on.

Teaching tip

When back at school, children can compare their maps, and the physical and human features of the local area can be displayed on an enlarged class map.

I love teaching about other countries, religions and cultures. From events like the Olympics and the World Cup, and even the nationalities of the children we teach, there are plenty of ideas when it comes to choosing a country to focus on. However, it is important that the children have a good understanding of their own local environment before they can *contrast* it – and the more personal, the better.

Provide the children with a map of your local town. As homework, ask them to identify where they live, the school and other places of interest. This might be the child's place of worship; local attractions, such as a museum, beach or monument; the football training grounds; their grandparents' house and so on. If looking at geographical features, the children could be asked to identify rivers, lakes, hills and town/city centres, for example. The map should be free for the children to add places of their choice. As shown in the quote above, one girl drew the route she takes to school.

Taking it further

Compare the children's maps with Google Earth. Is it easier to identify features on one map than the other?

Green for growth

'I'm going to climb my beanstalk.' Jack Lucas, age 3

A small seed can have enormous potential. Caring for a seed as it grows helps to develop a sense of responsibility and encourages children to raise questions about life and growing things.

Send each child home with one seed, a clear plastic cup, some kitchen towel and a set of instructions on how to get started. At home, the children need to put the damp piece of kitchen towel into the plastic cup with the seed pushed to the side, allowing it to be seen as it grows. Websites like Pinterest contain plenty of examples of what the cup should look like.

The activity is a brilliant way to watch germination as it happens, and can link well with so many science topics being taught in school.

Children should keep a diary, describing or drawing the seed as it changes from day to day, as well as keeping a table of measurements.

Questions to consider:

- What does the seed need to germinate?
- How does it get its energy?
- Where is the best place to keep the seed?
- Will the seed keep growing?

Teaching tip

Grow a beanstalk in school and film it using a time lapse camera. It is really useful watching the film back and pausing at key moments you want to focus on and discuss further.

Taking it further

Pupils can write instructions for younger children on how to grow a beanstalk and care for it.

It's good to be green

'It made me think about what we use all the different bins at home for.'

Many schools have a Green Team these days, who encourage more environmentally friendly habits around the school. Many schools hold a Green Week, with the whole school focusing on reducing, reusing and recycling. Including green-themed homework allows children to see that their environmental responsibilities extend beyond the school gates and it involves parents in school initiatives, too.

Environmentally friendly homework links well with learning in PSHE, citizenship, geography, science and even philosophy for children. It encourages children to think about their rights and responsibilities when it comes to the environment.

At home, children can record the ways in which they care for the environment by:

- listing some of the items/materials they recycle or reuse
- noting down water and electricity use – how can it be reduced?
- making a craft object or piece of art using recycled materials
- growing their own vegetables
- creating a 'Go Green' information leaflet, or a poster sharing tips.

Back in school, a class gallery can share ways in which the children are being 'green' at home.

Jobs in the community

'It really helped the children to recognise that people needed to make our community work.'

Local study projects in school help children to learn about their environments and communities beyond those of home and school, and can provide a fun and interesting homework challenge.

Links between PSHE and geography can be strengthened when thinking about the people whose jobs help us and others in our local area. As their homework task, ask the children to consider the local services and facilities they use (such as the doctor's surgery, their school, local leisure centre or library) and the people or jobs required for these jobs to exist.

Interestingly, the jobs may vary slightly, depending on where you live. For the children I teach, beach wardens and coast guards would be likely to make an appearance. Children in London may mention underground train drivers.

For younger children, providing a picture of a town and some of its facilities can be a good starting point. Older children can start thinking about the different sectors of the workforce and how each may contribute to the local economy.

The children can choose how they present their work, although I have found setting it out as a web or mind-map works well, as they can think of the facilities or services they use, and then stem off to think about the jobs involved.

Taking it further

Children could interview a family member about their job, devising questions that would enable them to share information about the role.

Bonus idea ★

Ask the children to speak to their parents about their role . . . as a parent. How does it compare to other jobs?

Outdoor treasure hunt

'A fun way to get families exploring the outdoors.'

Whatever the season, there is always so much to be explored in the outdoors. Providing the children with a simple scavenger hunt template is not only great fun, but also creates an opportunity for children to interact with their surroundings and can support a range of learning back in the classroom.

Outdoor scavenger hunts are particularly great for younger children, who are required to identify and name different plants, trees and common animals, and observe differences across the seasons.

Items to hunt for (or just 'spot') can include different coloured leaves, rocks, chestnuts, daffodils, pigeons, squirrels and so on. Items can vary depending on the time of year. As well as specific items, children can be asked to find natural items of different textures, shapes or colours.

Treasure hunts can also support other curriculum areas. Ask pupils to find something with an acute angle; made from at least two different materials; alive; or that is more than ten years old. Provide a list of things to hunt that are linked with various areas of your current curriculum.

Visit our home town

'This homework really supported learning of persuasive writing.'

When writing non-fiction, it is so important that the children are confident with the subject matter. Creating an advert for their local area not only requires the application of skills learnt in the classroom, but also asks the children to find out about (and appreciate) the best bits of their home towns!

Before setting the homework, spend some time in class finding out information about your local area. Tourist information and council websites are a great starting point. Once children have an idea of where to source information, and are familiar with the features of persuasive writing, ask them to create their own advert at home using the media of their choice.

Ask children to consider places such as particular landmarks, places to visit, things to do for families, restaurants and shopping areas.

I always find it helps to give the children an authentic audience. Get the local tourist office involved and explain to the children that their adverts will be displayed in their offices for visitors to read. This always enhances the quality of the work produced!

An alternative option is to produce an advert for the school, or for a lunchtime or after-school club that the children attend. These can be shared on the school website or blog for an audience interested in the school or local extra-curricular clubs.

Teaching tip

Provide a scaffold or list of required features to support children (and parents) in creating the adverts, without restricting their own choice too much.

Where in the world?

'Australia is massive!'

Locating the countries and continents of the world is a requirement of the English National Curriculum that can easily be explored in a range of creative ways, including through homework. Access to world maps online, as well as in atlases, makes it possible for all children to engage.

Younger children can be provided with a template of the world map and asked to find each continent and ocean. You may wish to provide the children with a list of continents and oceans for them to label.

Another option is for children to locate countries they have been to, or where their families live or come from. Some children might like to locate a country they would like to visit.

Access to Google Earth will enable older children to locate geographical features within particular countries, such as mountains, rivers or waterfalls. This also provides a good opportunity to start thinking about keys and symbols.

Maps by Aleksandra Mizielinska and Daniel Mizielinski and *City Atlas* by Martin Haake are both beautiful books to share with the class before setting more creative atlas work. Ask children to draw the outline of a particular country and then fill it with images that share some information about that country. These can make for stunning displays.

Map work is also useful for supporting maths. Ask the children to label different time zones, count the number of borders of a specific country, and even estimate the distance from the UK. Younger children could look at continents or particular countries and order them by size.

Bonus idea ★

Before setting map work, ask the children to have a go at drawing the British Isles or even a world map. The results are often 'interesting' and great for the children to look back on later and see their progress.

Weather diary

'This supported our learning about daily weather patterns tremendously.'

Everyday occurrences, like the weather, can provide fantastic stimuli back in the classroom. As well as learning about the physical geography of seasonal and daily weather patterns, weather data can support the application of learning in a range of other subjects. A simple task like keeping a daily weather diary at home can provide a great resource for the children back in school.

There are various ways to include weather as part of your students' homework. Ask them to watch the television weather forecast, or look it up online and compare it to the actual weather.

Provide a template or list of suggestions, asking the children to focus on the weather outside their homes. What can they feel, see and hear? Younger children can make a labelled drawing of the weather as they see it.

The www.bbc.co.uk/weather website provides a wide range of weather data, specifically linked to your particular area. Typing in the postcode, or town or city, brings up a forecast for the next ten days, including temperature, sunrise and sunset times, wind direction and wind speed. Ask the children to present this information in a table, linked with the data work you have been teaching in maths. By looking up the data of another country, the children can compare weather and find differences in temperature. This can be a particularly good way of looking at positive and negative numbers in context.

As well as just looking at the data, ask the pupils to plan a trip for somebody travelling from England to either a much colder or much warmer climate. What clothing and other accessories will be needed?

Teaching tip

The weather can also lend itself to creative writing. Ask the children to find examples of how the weather is used in literature to create atmosphere. Link it back to the use of figurative language in the classroom. Pie Corbett's 'The Day's Eye' is a fantastic poem about the sun. This can be adapted to thinking about a storm cloud, or thunder and lightning.

How can we improve our local area?

'This helped to promote a sense of citizenship and responsibility.'

Any class or homework on the theme of our local area can include asking the children to reflect on what they have seen, and then consider what improvements they would like. This leads to high quality conversations and follow-up work back in the classroom, as the children have seen first-hand areas they'd like to see improved.

After the children have had a chance to study their local area and consider some of its best features, ask them to think about ways in which they would like to see their towns improved. Ask the children to go for a walk around their local area, accompanied by an adult, and note down or photograph/sketch any particular area or equipment that they feel could be made better.

It is worth providing the children with some suggestions of things to look for before sending the work home. Ask the children to keep an eye out for things like:

- road signs and markings
- the road surface
- cycle lanes
- provision of bins
- dog litter or general litter in public places
- the condition of any play-park equipment
- unsightly graffiti
- designated road crossing areas.

Follow-up activities can include writing a persuasive letter to the local council, stating the areas that need improving and why, or creating a leaflet explaining to local people how they can support the area — for example, making sure dog litter is binned.

Bonus idea ★

Once back in school (or even before setting the homework), ask the children to give the school building and grounds a 'health check'. What could do with a lick of paint? Does the sensory garden need cutting back? Collect ideas and present them to the school council.

Stop, look and listen!

'Road safety is of vital importance.'

I have recently been working with our school council on the school's travel plan, thinking of ways to encourage families to walk to school, or at least park further out, so as to avoid congestion and potential accidents within our immediate surroundings. During one discussion, a school councillor mentioned that young children were not streetwise enough to walk to school. Whole-school homework activities have helped children become more confident pedestrians.

The 'Think!' road safety website (think.direct. gov.uk) states: 'Children will learn effectively if they receive the same clear safety instructions from home as from school, so it is vital that parents are encouraged to become involved with road safety from the beginning.' Involving parents through homework activities is one way we can ensure that this message is spread. The same website provides a wealth of lesson plans and home-link resources to share with families.

Ask children to look out for and research pedestrian road signs. Can they explain what they mean, as well as draw some out? A simple template could be put together to support this.

Ask children to draw their route to school, identifying potential hazards and finding the safest places to cross roads if necessary. What road signs do they come across on their way to and from school?

Children can create road safety or Highway Code posters and information leaflets to be discussed and displayed back in school. The best of these can be distributed to parents or laminated and displayed near school parking zones.

> **Bonus idea** ★
>
> Get the children thinking about how their clothing can protect them on the roads. For homework, ask them to draw themselves with appropriate clothing that will help to keep them safe while out walking or cycling.

TECHNOLOGY

Part 8

100-word challenge

'The unread story is not a story; it is little black marks on wood pulp. The reader, reading it, makes it live: a live thing, a story.'
Ursula K. Le Guin

The 100-word challenge website provides a weekly prompt, which can be a picture, a short sentence or a series of individual words, and the children can use up to 100 words to write a creative piece.

Teaching tip

It's always good to give back, so I make sure my children comment on the work of others, giving positive feedback as well as any Even Better If . . . (EBI . . .) pointers! The children love this just as much as the challenge itself!

I am always referring to purpose and audience when it comes to children's writing. Anyone who has attended any of my English training sessions will know it! This is why I was delighted when I came across the weekly 100-word challenge. I ask children to do this as their homework, and upload it onto our class blog. I then add the links to the website https://100wc.net/ (although, with some training, older children are able to do this themselves). The beauty of the site is that each piece of work is commented on, usually by someone from a different part of the country or even the world.

The children are always amazed when they see they have feedback from somebody in Australia or Mexico or even London! The flag counter on our blog shows thousands of hits from around the world, and the impact of having a global audience has been immense, particularly as the children are keen to have error-free work!

A world of tech

'It's not that we use technology, we live technology.' Godfrey Reggio

Student teachers often gasp in disbelief when I speak of life as a teacher pre interactive whiteboards and Google Drive. I occasionally hear older teachers speak of a Banda photocopier – I'm still not entirely sure what that is! Understanding the use of technology and the benefits it can offer, as well as thinking about how we might live without it, is worth investigating.

Ask the children to investigate the technology used at home by themselves and their family members. The vast majority of homes will have a kettle, microwave, television and washing machine, with many also having hairdryers, computers, tablets and Wi-Fi.

This homework links well with learning about electricity, as the children can consider how the items are powered and the reasons for their inventions. How do they make life at home easier? What would people have done before these items were available? What would they do in the event of a power cut?

Children can list the electrical items, their purpose and what could be used as a non-electrical alternative. They could also ask what items were around when their parents or grandparents were younger! As the older children hand in their mobile phones each morning, they find it amazing that I didn't have a mobile phone until my 18th birthday. My grandmother still doesn't own one!

Taking it further

Looking at the electric meter could link nicely to the Number hunt (Idea 24) homework activity. How much electricity does your family use over the space of a week? How is electricity measured?

Padlet

'I've added a link to a really good website to our class Padlet.'

If you have never used Padlet, you must! I first came across Padlet on Twitter, where many users post links to one in order to collect ideas. From children's picture books to art in the classroom, Padlet has been an invaluable resource, and is brilliant to use with the children, too.

In layman's terms, Padlet (padlet.com) allows users to add suggestions, upload photos or provide weblinks. I have seen it used numerous times via Twitter to share ideas amongst teachers. Recently I created a Padlet to collect examples of artwork that can be used in the primary classroom. It didn't take me long to set one up and start using it in the classroom with the children. After sharing the link with the children, I encouraged them to share any useful information or ideas for a class topic or homework on the platform.

Ideas for using Padlet:

- class book reviews (upload a picture of the book with a summary and own opinions)
- YouTube links (I have shared links for some great science videos for the children to check out as part of their homework)
- compliment corner (create a page where children can write an online comment complimenting or thanking someone in the class)
- 'I wonder' questions (after introducing a topic, ask children to list any questions they have these can be referred to back in the classroom, or answered by other pupils via the Padlet)
- philosophy for children (also known as P4C) (post a question and ask children to think about it at home, or even provide their own questions to get the class thinking).

Bonus idea ★

Voice recordings can easily be attached to a class Padlet, allowing you to provide instructions or information orally. Children can also upload their own recordings. This has worked brilliantly with children learning performance poetry as a homework activity.

Time online

'As a parent it made me consider the amount of time we all spend online.'

The Internet is undoubtedly an incredible resource, offering a magnitude of information at our fingertips. Online games and the rise of social media mean our pupils are spending more time than ever online, and it is useful for them to be aware of this.

Have you ever had to teach when the entire computer network at school had gone down, or the photocopier was out of order, or the PowerPoint presentation you prepared at home just wasn't compatible with the software at school? This actually happened to a friend of mine at her interview for her current job. With no alternative, she turned to 'naked teaching', a term coined by Nina Jackson when referring to tech-free classrooms – returning to the basics.

Primary pupils today won't remember life at school without many of today's mod cons. For the majority, the use of the Internet will be the norm. Whether it be through their parents' email, online shopping, use of social media or the range of online games many primary-aged pupils enjoy playing, life with Wi-Fi will be considered an essential commodity.

I tend to begin each half term's computing lessons with an e-safety input. For homework, ask the children to keep a record of their online use.

- What online games do you play?
- Which apps do you use?
- Which websites do you visit?
- How do you stay safe online?
- How else is the Internet used in your home?
- What would you do/use if the Internet was not around?

> **Teaching tip**
>
> Provide links to some educational websites/games that children can play at home and which will support curriculum learning.

> **Bonus idea**
>
> Before setting the homework, speak with the children about online use within the classroom. Many teaching tools require Internet access, but what could we use instead, if required?

App review

'A great pre-coding activity.'

Since the publication of the new English Primary National Curriculum, coding in the classroom has gone through the roof. One of the activities I do with older primary pupils is to design and create an exam revision app. But before this can happen, I want the children to explore other educational apps and assess what makes them useful . . . or not.

Before setting this homework, explore apps regularly used in the classroom. Discuss what makes having certain apps on our phones or tablets so beneficial. Share some of your favourite or most-used apps and ask the children to do the same.

At home, ask the children to spend time exploring an educational app. Once they are familiar with the content and layout, ask them to list the app's best features, what could make it better and how it might support their learning, plus a general comment and star rating. It might be worthwhile providing a template if you think your students will require one.

Once back in school, and ready to start planning their own apps, the children will hopefully have gained an idea of what they need to include in their own educational apps.

Bonus idea ★

Phil Bagge's www.code-it.co.uk website is full of resources to support classroom computing teaching using Scratch. Many of my pupils have been so inspired that they have carried on with projects at home. Touch Develop also provides 'Hour of Code' tutorials, which children can complete at home on a PC. Both provide fantastic introductions to the world of coding.

Typing skills

'The need for teaching the basic skills hasn't gone.'

During a #PrimaryRocks chat one Monday evening, many people expressed how the computing curriculum in primary schools had become all about coding. I too had noticed how some of my ten- and eleven-year-old students were struggling with basic word-processing skills, and my planning has since been tweaked! But homework also provides a perfect opportunity (for older children in particular) to practise these skills.

Two really great websites to improve typing skills are www.typingclub.com and the BBC's Dance Mat Typing. These provide activities that help the children become familiar with the layout of a keyboard, and quick-fire tasks against the clock soon help the children speed up!

Word-processing software contains many features that most of take for granted, but it is important that the children become familiar and confident users, in order to have the option of presenting work in a variety of ways, and for different levels of formality.

Give the children a copy of a favourite poem. Ask them to type it up for homework, following a specific set of instructions. These might include:

- Centralise the title and poet's name.
- Type the title in bold type and the poet's name in italics.
- Select a font that you feel suits the poem.
- Set the font size to 12 and line spacing to 1.5.
- Find any words or phrases you would like to magpie (verb: to steal shiny ideas!) and type them in another colour.
- Insert a picture from the web that will suit the poem.

Bonus idea

My current school is set up with Google Classroom, so pupils are able to share their work with me and I am able to provide a quick comment. Exemplary homework can be easily accessed and shared with the children when back in the classroom. This is a real bonus, as the children do not need to print their work or bring it in on a not-so-trusty USB stick!

Flow charts

'A great pre-coding homework activity.'

Before children begin learning to code in the classroom, it is worth spending time thinking about the basics. Coding is a step-by-step guide for the computer to complete a task. This task and its variations will help children to understand the importance of giving accurate instructions.

An option for younger children, or as an initial homework task, is to provide them with a maze. Ask them to draw the route through the maze and then write out the instructions that would allow somebody else to work their way through it. This will obviously involve lots of *turn left*, *turn right* and *straight on* vocabulary. Ask the children to think of examples where they hear similar language – many may be used to hearing a satnav.

Moving on from this, ask the children to complete a flowchart for a simple activity that they complete regularly, such as waking up and getting ready for school, walking to the local park or making a cup of tea.

Provide children with the details of each flowchart symbol, including start/stop, process and decision. Include an example that the children can refer to for support.

Back in school, children can share their flowcharts and evaluate how effective they are with a partner. As you move on to looking at inputting code, hopefully the children will see the relationship. Programs like Scratch are great for early coders, as the blocked scripts can be easily compared to a flowchart. It is also worth asking the children to input the code for their original mazes to enable getting 'Scratch' through successfully.

Taking it further

Coding instructions link really well with maths and English. Tie in this idea with learning about angles and instructional writing, and get the children up and moving to test out instructions for getting from one room to another, or from the classroom out to the playground.

E-safety

'E-safety helmets must be worn.'

The children I teach find it incredible to believe that I once lived in a world without Facebook, Instagram or Snapchat. Although I sometimes wonder if my own teenage years were easier because of an absence of social media, I also recognise the benefits and opportunities it provides for people in their everyday lives. The important factor here is to ensure that our young people are capable users, aware of the possible threats and pitfalls of the online world.

Schools regularly hold e-safety information sessions for parents, although if your school is anything like many others, a lot of parents will attend, but not *all* of them. By setting e-safety homework from a young age, parents at home can get involved and understand some of the issues.

Ask the children to discuss some of the potential dangers of online use with their families. They can make a list of the dangers and add how they ensure they keep themselves safe. This could include keeping passwords safe, keeping social media accounts private, only chatting with people they know and thinking before they post!

It is worth sharing some websites that the children can explore with their families to enable them to consider the various hazards.

Once the information has been collated, ask the children to create an e-safety poster or leaflet that can be shared in school. This can always be set as a competition, with the winning entries distributed across the school.

Teaching tip

It is important to ensure that the homework task does not replace any e-safety lessons in school. The homework is a way of getting the children to think about computer safety at home with their families.

Taking it further

With more and more primary children also having their own mobile phones, it is worth including texting and photos in class and home discussions as well.

Film review

'A great excuse to curl up with some popcorn.'

Writing a film review is often a welcome piece of homework over the winter holidays when the weather is unlikely to be great. If it can coincide with any film work going on at school, then even better.

Taking it further

Display film reviews in the library close to where the book version is available. Ask children to compare the film and book.

A fantastic site full of resources to support the teaching of film is www.intofilm.org. If you don't currently have a film club, it may be something you would like to look into, as it works brilliantly as an extra-curricular club.

Over a school holiday, ask the children, if they manage to watch a film, to write up a review that can be shared back in school, or even on the intofilm website. Before the children watch the film, ask them to consider:

- What is your favourite type of film and why?
- What do you already know about the film you are about to watch?
- What type of film is it? (Action, adventure, comedy)
- What do you think the film is about?

Once the children have watched the film, they can comment on the plot, the main characters, the best bits, what surprised them and what they didn't like, and give it a star rating. If linking with film work back in school, provide a word-bank for the children to use, including terminology such as: *sound effects, soundtrack, setting, camera, lighting* and *mood*.

Bonus idea ★

Share reviews on the class webpage to recommend holiday viewing to other children.

Younger children may just want to think about character and setting. Ask them to draw their favourite character and write descriptive sentences or draw a picture of their favourite scene.

Genius hour

'Genius hour – where passions come alive.'

I was first introduced to 'genius hour' by Graham Andre, editor of the Maths Shed, at a TeachMeet I hosted in Bournemouth. Providing an hour per week, plus setting the project as homework, allows children time to explore their own passions.

Genius hour doesn't need to rely on technology, but can link brilliantly with it. During a recent computing topic, focusing on presenting information in a variety of ways, I hooked the students in by allowing them to present on a topic of *their* choice. Computing skills were, of course, the main focus, along with research and presentation skills, but the actual content was entirely up to the children.

Being set up with Google Classroom made it a lot easier, as pupils were able to access their materials in school and at home with simply a login and password. Topics varied from Manchester United to Alex Rider books, and from gymnastic sports to rock climbing.

Encourage children to include links to webpages, video and picture inserts, animation effects (although these should probably be limited!) and anything else that has been a focus in your computing teaching.

Teaching tip

In true genius hour style, the children would be allowed to choose how their project was presented.

Taking it further

Once the children are confident in using the computing software, it could be applied to enhance learning in other curriculum areas as well.

FINDING OUT

Part 9

Interviews

'Can I ask you a question?'

Children often laugh (or, dare I say, scoff!) when they hear about how things used to be. But encouraging discussions with parents and grandparents can be a real learning opportunity for discovering the 'past'.

Taking it further

Grandparents or relatives with particular experiences are often willing to come into class to share these and take questions. Obviously, being aware of the sensitivity of any experiences, it is often worth asking.

Children's engagement is often increased when they get the chance to speak to somebody who experienced something first hand. Our ten- and eleven-year-old children were fortunate enough to speak to a man who experienced WWII and was able to describe his childhood at that time. We all know what a difference such opportunities makes compared with reading about it in a book.

The children's older relatives are also a very useful resource and can support the wider class' understanding of the past, in their local areas and beyond. Specific interview questions can tell them a lot about what life was like in the past, and allow them to compare the childhoods of people from different countries as well.

Questions might include:

- When/where were you born? What's your earliest memory?
- Who are the oldest relatives you remember? What were they like?
- What was your school like? Describe the teachers. What subjects did you learn?
- What was your first job?
- Tell me about your wedding day.
- What were your hobbies?
- What was life like without computers/mobile phones/the Internet?
- What festivals did you celebrate? How?
- What is your message to young people today?

Supermarket sweep

'Going to Sainsbury's was actually fun!'

Parents of young children everywhere understand the need to keep their little darlings occupied whilst rushing around the supermarket. Actually, the supermarket provides a wealth of learning opportunities that can support learning in school.

Ask children to go to the supermarket equipped with a notepad and pencil, ready to complete some of the following activities:

- Alphabet shopping: create an A–Z list of objects you can buy at the supermarket. This develops children's knowledge of different foods.
- List the fruit and vegetables you bought. How many of each did you buy? Children can create different charts showing the number of fruit/vegetables bought.
- What items are kept in the fridge?
- Look at the 'best before' date on an item you bought. How long will it stay fresh for?
- Can you find at least five different countries of origin when you look at the packaging? What does this tell us? Can you find the countries on a map?
- Can you organise the food shopping into the different food groups?

Teaching tip

This homework links particularly well with topics about 'Where our food comes from'. The children's discoveries can be shared on a large world map. Whole-class tally charts can show which fruits and vegetables are the most popular.

Bonus idea ★

In the age of the Internet, it is worth noting that many families will buy online. Children can explore food groups and find an A–Z list on the supermarket's webpage.

What's in the news?

'I didn't really know much about what was happening in the world before.'

Using current affairs in the classroom is an excellent way of providing purpose to the children's learning. News clips and newspaper articles offer wonderful stimuli and are great for hooking the children in to learning. Encouraging the children to find out what is happening in the world, or even just the local area, can develop not only reading skills, but also an overall awareness of life beyond their everyday experiences.

Teaching tip

Many newspapers have online versions that children can use if access to real newspapers is limited. Alternatively, many public libraries now stock children's newspapers too. *First News* offers subscriptions for schools, and comes with a wealth of online resources.

Bonus idea ★

Enjoy some creative writing back in class by asking the children to share chosen headlines from home with classmates. Get the children to write up the article, based only on the headline. They can be as entertaining as you wish, but should keep to the style of journalistic writing. This can, of course, be reversed so that the children write the headline for a given article.

Many schools subscribe to children's newspapers or, like my school, have the children produce their own. There is an infinite number of ways to use the articles from children's newspapers, both in the classroom and as homework.

- The simplest idea is to send an article home (or ask the children to find their own, with help from a parent to ensure suitability) and ask the children to write a very short synopsis in their reading diaries.
- Select a headline and work out what the article is about (before reading it).
- Cut out a selection of headlines and bring them into school for the class to work out the story.
- Have a go at writing the story to go with a given headline.
- If learning about the features of a newspaper in school, ask the children to identify the features within a newspaper at home.
- Go on a newspaper treasure hunt. Find a good news story, a bad news story, a weather forecast, an article about a politician, an article about a sports star, a job advert and a favourite piece (and explain why!).

I wonder . . .

'Providing question stems was really useful.'

When first planning a new topic, there are obviously school curriculum objectives that must be covered, but it is also worthwhile finding out what the children would like to know. This task works well both in class and as a homework task.

Introduce the children to a new topic. This works particularly well with subjects like science, history and geography units. A hook and some basic information can be a good start. For homework, ask the children to create a list of 'I wonder' statements or questions. Providing a list of question stems is an ideal prompt: *what, where, why, how, when, which, if.* For a previous topic I taught on space, the children returned to school with a variety of 'I wonder' statements.

I wonder . . .

- Why Pluto is no longer a planet?
- How far we are from the sun?
- When how long it takes to orbit the sun was discovered?
- Why we have different seasons?
- How old space is?
- Why there is no gravity in space?

As part of the children's homework, ask them to find the answer to at least three of their questions.

Back in school, display the questions on a working wall and ask the children to add the answers as the topic progresses. Providing children with the opportunity to ask some of their own questions gives them a little ownership over their learning.

> **Teaching tip**
>
> I often ask the children for their 'first ideas' in the classroom, before setting the 'I wonder' homework. Ask the children to mind-map everything they think they already know about a particular topic. This highlights any misconceptions that need correcting during the topic and is a great way to inform your planning.

Supporting charity

'This helped the children to realise they can make a difference.'

Many children will not understand the concept of 'charity' or the role of a charitable organisation. Through PSHE and exploring your local communities, encourage the children to find out about local organisations and how they can help to raise awareness.

Taking it further

Research a charity affiliated with the school, or find one for the school to support. Children, particularly those in the school council, can plan initiatives to raise money and awareness for the charity.

Bonus idea ★

Ask the children to design and make something that can be sold at a school fair to raise money for a charity. This is great for developing enterprise skills as well.

This homework task is ideally suited to children in the upper years of primary school, although it could be tweaked to suit others. Ask the children to research and find out about a local charity, ready to present back to their classmates. This may be a charity that they and their families already support, or it might involve some Internet research.

Provide some prompts to support the children in their research. They could be asked to include:

- the charity's logo
- the history and aims of the charity
- what they do to raise money
- how others can support the charity.

This homework task links well with many areas of learning within PSHE, but also supports citizenship, British Values and supporting our local areas. Children will develop an awareness of others in need and the power they have to make a difference.

Inspirational people

'Studying those who have overcome their own hardships is great for promoting a growth mindset.'

With so many schools now aware of promoting 'growth mindset' and encouraging resilience amongst children, it is worth looking at examples of people who walk the talk – people who genuinely have not given up in times of adversity. Different people are inspirational to different people – ask the children who their role models are and why.

Many successful people have stated how their failures have been a step towards their own success. Before setting the homework, discuss the term 'role model' and what it means to be inspirational. Look at examples like Thomas Edison, who carried out 2,000 experiments before finally inventing the electric light bulb. When Edison was asked about failing so many times, he replied, 'Failing? I did not fail. I invented the electric light bulb. It just happened to be a 2,000 step process.'

At home, ask the children to think carefully about someone who has succeeded, despite facing challenges. This could be a famous person or someone the child knows personally.

Ask them to answer:

- What has this person achieved?
- What challenges were in their way?
- How did they overcome these obstacles?
- What do you think this person said to themselves when they felt like quitting?
- Who might have helped them?

Allow children to choose how they present their findings but be prepared for the next lesson to think about and discuss their role model.

Teaching tip

It is sometimes worth providing a list of names that children can choose from and research. This works well with particular topics, or when thinking about current news events.

Family tree

'It showed how family is so much more than just the people we live with!'

At a recent family event, the adults among us were put to the test by my niece, who wanted to know what everybody's relation was to one another. It started off relatively easy to explain until we got into the complexities of second cousins and great aunts and uncles!

Children are naturally curious about family members. It took a while for my daughter to understand that I have parents and siblings too. I remember her telling me how my mum was actually called 'Gran', as though I'd called her by the wrong name!

Ask children to draw their immediate families in the form of a family tree. With a little help, ask them to draw in their extended family. Providing a family tree of a famous family (possibly the Royals) is a good way to demonstrate how one works. It is also important to bear in mind the dynamics of some families and ensure that the homework is not going to make anyone feel uncomfortable. As the children's teacher, you will know best how to set this type of homework.

Allow the children to choose how they present their family tree. Some may simply want to write in the names whereas others will be keen to draw pictures or stick in photographs. Encourage the children to be creative, as it can make a fabulous family keepsake when the homework is complete.

Library scavenger hunt

'We signed up as members the same day.'

I love nothing better than a visit to the local library. My own children also love it as they know that no item is too expensive! Sharing the awe and wonder of a library with the children we teach is so important, and a few homework activities that encourage a visit are well worth the effort.

Provide a list of things for the children to find on their scavenger hunt at the library. They must record the details. You might include:

- a picture book
- a chapter book
- a magazine or comic
- a DVD
- a book about space (or another topic)
- a book by an author with a surname beginning with 'L'
- a new arrival
- the information desk
- an activity taking place at the library.

For older children, it is worth them becoming familiar with the Dewey Decimal System. Provide a list of classification numbers and ask the children to find a book from that section.

Encourage the children to borrow some books linked with their interests or a topic being learnt in school.

Taking it further

Ask the children to design a poster that encourages others to visit their school or local library. These can be sent to the library or displayed in school.

Health and safety audit

'It made us all aware of possible dangers in the home.'

As teachers, we are all aware of health and safety procedures in school, like the fire exit route or risk assessments for off-site visits or those more extreme science experiments! This task asks children and their families to carry out a health and safety audit of their own homes.

This homework works well if set alongside a whole-school Safety Week, or if linked to learning in PSHE, where the children are exploring the meaning of hazards and how to prevent them.

Once in-class teaching has covered 'safety in the home', it is a worthwhile opportunity to get the children to carry out some checks of their own!

Ask the children to draw a plan of their kitchen, including doors and windows, electrical items and appliances, as well as cupboards and drawers. List potential hazards, thinking about what is kept in cupboards (chemical products and sharp objects). What can be done to minimise risks?

Older children can draw a plan of their homes, marking out fire escape routes and noting any other potential hazards, like pets, the stairs, the bathroom or the garage.

Teaching tip

If the homework follows on from the learning in school, it will be more meaningful and accessible for the children. They will be aware of the different hazards in the home and so they will be easier to identify and share with their families.

Bonus idea ★

Ask children to share and discuss the fire escape route with their family members and display it somewhere prominent. Knowing where they should go (an agreed muster point like a neighbour's house) and who to call is also useful for the children to know!

Murder mystery

'The whole family got involved!'

Detective work is hugely popular with both adults and children. Detective fiction is a thriving genre, both in the bookshops and on radio and television. Murder mysteries, or similar detective activities, provide a range of skills that benefit children greatly.

Many subjects can be supported through practising detective skills, and a good murder mystery provides a fun homework task for the whole family. Science skills, including observing, predicting, recording data and concluding, are supported through detective activities. Using evidence to answer questions is also beneficial to subjects like history and geography.

Set a murder mystery, or an alternative detective task, for the children to solve at home. Reading skills are of huge importance in order to gather the information correctly. Allow the children to choose how they go about recording their findings – the process is often very interesting to look back on.

A quick Google search will provide a wealth of murder mysteries ready to be used with primary-aged children, or have a go at making your own! Linking a mystery to a topic you are currently teaching provides cross-curricular opportunities, too. Saviour Pirotta's *Ancient Greek Mysteries* are great for getting the children predicting and working out the various crimes, as well as giving insight into life in Ancient Greece.

Taking it further

Murder mysteries work brilliantly as reading comprehensions. *Give two reasons why the inspector came to the conclusion . . . What led the police to believe . . .? Explain why you think . . . What do you think the letter said?*

Bonus idea ★

Set the murder mystery as a homework task while studying the detective fiction-writing genre. Once the children have solved the mystery at home, they can write up the story to go with it, describing how the crime was solved.

LEARNING
NUGGETS

Part 10

Talking homework

'Talk is the sea upon which all else floats.' James Britton

If a child cannot think or say something, how can we expect them to write it? This homework task is an excellent way to involve families in their children's learning and save time in the classroom! As well as this, it encourages language and oracy and is of huge benefit to all children.

Teaching Tip

Ensure talking homework doesn't become an easy alternative to more traditional homework. In order for it to be effective, families need to be on board and understand its role in supporting class learning.

Provide the children with a question or topic to discuss at home in preparation for a class discussion or writing task the following day. By having these conversations at home, the children return to school brimming with ideas and eager to share with their classmates. The classroom becomes a hothouse of ideas and suggestions, which, of course, can be magpied *(copied)* or discussed further. Having time to orally rehearse at home, and take on suggestions from family members, allows the children to come into school prepared for the lesson ahead.

In order for talking homework to be successful, I would recommend including its premise in a session with new parents, and possibly at the start of each school year, so that parents are aware of its value and ways in which they can support it. A slip of paper or a note in the homework diary explaining the talking homework is also important.

Examples of talking homework tasks I have used are:

- You wake up to discover you have a super power. What is it and how do you use it to good effect?
- Should the council build on our green land? (*I linked this to a story in our local news. Provide information about proposals to build new homes on local green space and the*

effects it might have on animals and habitats, traffic, local people and so on.)

- If I were the Prime Minister, I would . . . because . . .
- The best children's book of the year is . . . because . . .

It is worth providing a bank of sentence-starters that children (and their families) should aim to include in their conversations. The more the children orally rehearse the vocabulary and phrases from their cue cards, the more likely they will be to start including it within their writing.

Talking homework really can support learning in any subject, as well as significantly improve oracy skills amongst the children. Provide the children with a painting or portrait of a particular person, and ask them to describe what they can see as part of their family conversation. Ask them to discuss their upcoming science experiment and make predictions based on known facts. They could even describe their favourite (or dream) holiday – what made it so special?

Plenty of suggestions for talking homework are shared online, often via school websites. A Google search should get you started, although linking it to the learning taking place in school will ensure it is not just an add-on!

Just as you would in the class, ask families to come up with some rules for group talking. They might consider where they sit when the conversation takes place, how they show they are actively listening, and how they ensure everybody's voice is heard. The children can share some of their home talk rules when back in school.

Teaching Tip

Allow children to rehearse feeding back their homework in pairs or small groups before moving on to any whole class discussions. This, along with suggesting the children refer to any notes they might have made, will lead to a more proactive discussion where you will see the ideas flow.

Bonus idea

Model talking homework for parents, either during an information event or as a recording that can be shared on your school's website. This can be a real help to families who might struggle with questioning techniques or encouraging their children to participate, and resort to just giving their own ideas!

Talking homework is a great way to develop ideas for extended writing, as well as subjects like philosophy for children (P4C), where there is not necessarily a right or wrong answer, but the children need to be prepared to justify their views.

Poll it

'Do you think there is life in outer space?'

One way of getting pupils interested in current affairs is to hold a weekly poll asking for viewpoints on a controversial topic. Providing some background information and a key question to ponder over as homework sets up the thinking ready for being back in class.

Encourage children to explore the issue at home with parents or other family members. As well as reading the information provided, can they research any further pieces that can help them come to a decision? This is a perfect example of Talking homework (see Idea 91), as family discussion is highly encouraged.

You will find that, once back in the classroom, pupils are prepared to share their viewpoint with evidence or reasons/justification to support their opinions.

If you do sign up to *First News*, you will find that you are able to send in the results of your poll to the newspaper, including any particular quotes from the children. The number of votes for or against is published in the following week's edition, as well as some chosen quotes. I have had a few pupils' quotes published and, I can tell you, their reactions are priceless!

Alternatively, display the results of any polls, along with quotes explaining why, up on your classroom wall, ready to be considered by others.

Words you need to know

'A man with a scant vocabulary will almost certainly be a weak thinker.' Henry Hazlitt

Most vocabulary is learnt through hearing it spoken, or by reading it, but many subjects require it to be specifically taught. Setting vocabulary homework not only improves children's understanding and spelling of the words, but also makes it more likely to be applied within classroom writing.

At the start of each topic or theme, I give the children a list of key vocabulary within a table (an idea that I picked up from Jennifer Hart, a deputy head and science teacher at an education conference in 2015). Next to the specific vocabulary, the table contains four columns titled:

1 *Words I don't know*
2 *Words I've heard of but don't know the meaning of*
3 *Words I know the meaning of*
4 *Definition*

Complete the table in class initially. Words already known can easily be filled in, then ask the children to find out more about the unknown words at home. This can include spelling practice to enable the word to be more easily applied when back in class.

In addition, ask the children to create a bookmark at home, listing key vocabulary for subjects like science, or a specific history or geography topic. These can be designed however the children choose, and then used back in school to mark the page in their class books. This means the children have easy access to spellings of key terminology when writing, and also makes marking easier as the bookmark should be left on the last piece of work!

Taking it further

Provide the National Curriculum spelling list at the start of each year, explaining to children and parents what it is! Include a couple of words at random in each spelling test, and ask children to look out for the words in their reading.

Bonus idea ★

Ask children to create their own crosswords or word searches to share with children back in school.

Jeopardy

'One of my favourite quiz shows!'

Following on from Words you need to know (Idea 93), a fun game to play at home (as well as in the classroom) is Jeopardy. Those of you familiar with the gameshow will know how the game can help to deepen understanding of vocabulary, as well as key people and events in history or world news.

Taking it further

Provide one answer and ask the children to list as many questions as they can that would give the answer. This involves some creative thinking! For example, providing a colour, a number, a country or a famous person as an answer can involve numerous questions.

Bonus idea ★

Playing Jeopardy can link nicely with Idea 83 – What's in the news? – as it encourages children to find the questions to each answer. In the past, I have given the answers 'Duchess of Cambridge', 'refugees' and 'Brazil' and asked the children to write questions, based on their reading of that week's news, that would result in the answer provided.

Jeopardy is a game show with a twist, as players are given the answers to which they must provide the questions. For example, if the children have the answer 'Earth', they might ask, 'What is the name of the planet we live on?'

Giving the answers based on key history vocabulary or people and places can support knowledge and understanding back in the classroom. 'Samuel Pepys', 'Pudding Lane', 'bakery' and '1666' are examples of the answers I could give to the children during a 'Great Fire of London' topic. At home, children can write a question for each answer. During a science topic on space, I might give the answers '24 hours', 'leap year', 'summer', 'Pluto', 'night' and '365.25 days'.

Once the children have created their questions, it can be a fun game to play with the family, or even back in school as a lesson starter! It is also worth taking time to check and correct any misconceptions.

Bingo!

'The parents love it just as much as the children!'

This classic game can be applied to learning in literally any subject.

Bingo is a great starter or plenary activity, which can provide an opportunity to practise and refer back to knowledge of terminology or serve as mental maths practice. Once the children are familiar with the format in school, it is an easy homework task to set. It works well as ongoing homework, so it is worth making sure parents know how it works.

Ask parents to play a game of bingo with the children based on a multiplication table you are currently learning (or to keep up practice of others!) or on number bonds to 10 or 20. With the example of tables, ask the children to list six multiples of 8 on a grid. The parents, or a helping sibling, can call out calculations, e.g. 4 x 8, and the child crosses off a bingo square if they have 32. Once all six squares have been crossed, the child calls 'bingo'.

An alternative version is to provide a word bank with definitions linked to learning in a particular subject. This could be measurement vocabulary or linked with a space topic, for example. The child can choose six of the words and only cross them off once the definition for each word has been read out. Practised regularly, this improves children's use of vocabulary back in the classroom.

Younger children can play bingo with high-frequency words, crossing out each word once it's read. Regular practice allows children to become familiar with reading words they will often come across.

> **Teaching tip**
>
> Websites like Twinkl have ready-made bingo resources to save you time! A blank template can easily be filled with hand-written words and photocopied.

> **Bonus idea**
>
> Provide a choice of homework activities on a bingo grid. This works well with reading homework. Each week, the children can choose a different activity to complete. These might include listing new words, drawing a picture of a character or writing a short review.

Hidden homework

'Brainteasers are a great disguise for homework!'

Brainteasers, jokes and riddles are great fun but also provide opportunities to problem-solve and think critically and creatively.

Brainteasers and riddles often require us to think in unconventional ways. Reading the problem carefully is essential to pick up on any clues. The Internet has an abundance of riddles and brainteasers to suit different age groups, which can often be included as a fun 'extra' or as a main task if a little more meaty.

Maths riddles are particularly great. Simple ones include examples such as 'How can you add eight 8s to obtain the answer 1000?' *(888+88+8+8+8=1000)*, while more complex ones might involve the children needing to draw out patterns or diagrams. Many people will remember the 'Teresa's daughter' riddle that did the rounds on social media recently. If not, type it into Google and go for it! For many, the only way to solve it was to draw out a kind of family tree!

Cryptology and code activities can link well with maths and history topics. Ask the children to write a message in Morse code or using Egyptian hieroglyphics, to be solved by a friend back in school.

Detective puzzles and murder mysteries also require problem-solving and reasoning skills. Ask the children to make up their own once they have solved some and got the idea.

Bonus idea ★

Ask children to find a joke (or write their own) that can be shared back in school. My previous head teacher used to always end his assemblies with a joke, often provided by the children.

Magpie book

'Writers act like thieves. They are constantly raiding their lives for ideas.' Pie Corbett

As a strong advocate of Talk 4 Writing (an approach to teaching writing developed by Pie Corbett), I am a huge fan of the magpie book! Just like a magpie who is on the prowl for shiny, bright objects, a writer steals all the best words and phrases they come across. As I tell the children I teach, special words don't belong to anyone in particular — they are free for us all to use.

At the start of the school year, supply each child with a small exercise book, which is to become their magpie book. These can be covered in shiny foil to make them even more special! Encourage the children to take these books home with them and keep them close, especially whilst reading.

When the children come across a word or phrase that is worthy of stealing, they need to write it down in their magpie books, as this can then be referred to throughout independent writing. Any spectacular magpies can also be shared on the class magpie board.

This is an ongoing homework task, which pupils can be filling in throughout the year. Encourage pupils to ensure they have their book with them in school, too, as it is a particularly useful resource during shared reading and writing.

Teaching tip

If the children have reading diaries, this can be used to store magpie words as part of their weekly homework, in place of a separate magpie book.

Taking it further

Ask the children to write down magpie terminology from other curriculum areas that will be useful to their writing. This could be specific vocabulary for subjects like science, geography, history or RE.

Loop card dominoes

'A fun way of practising skills and memorising key information.'

Loop cards are regularly used in the classroom and work well used with the whole class to ensure that all children are listening and to avoid missing their responses. A simple set of loop cards can also support learning at home.

Taking it further

Set the children the challenge of creating their own loop cards, using a given template. Laminate these and keep them as a classroom resource. Playing them as a game of dominoes is another wet-play option!

There is no doubt that loop cards are best played with a large group of people. One card is usually enough, two at a push.

Free loop card resources are available online, or you can create your own using a loop card generator site. At home, the loop cards can be played like dominoes, with family or alone. You might ask the children to stick the game down so that it can be referred to in later homework tasks, or kept as a game that can be played time and time again.

The best thing about loop cards is that they can support so many curriculum areas. Mental maths calculations are the most obvious – they are ideal for practising number bonds or times tables – but they are also great for shape work ('I am a 2D shape with three equal sides and three equal angles' = 'I am an equilateral triangle').

Loop cards are also fantastic for learning SPaG terminology. Put the term on one card and the definition on another ('I take the place of a noun, e.g. **I** live in London, **She** is my friend' = 'pronoun'). Eventually line all of the cards up in the style of dominoes.

Topic information can also be rehearsed, such as key people or dates in history or capital cities and languages of the world.

Gobblefunk

'What a splendiferous activity!'

This idea stems from a game I bought called 'Gobblefunk', based, of course, on the splendiferous vocabulary of the BFG. The game works similarly to Balderdash and is a great way of working on vocabulary for any subject.

This activity works well as a lesson starter or as a homework option to reinforce key vocabulary and its meanings. Provide a word alongside three definitions, only one of which is correct. The children need to choose which definition is correct and put the word into a sentence, or find an example in a piece of writing.

It works brilliantly for SPaG, as it is a fun way of becoming familiar with the terminology and can be played on a regular basis, even linking to other subjects.

Examples:

Sphinx

- Noun: a mythical creature with the head of a human and the body of a lion.
- Adjective: soft to touch.
- Verb: to kill somebody with a spear.

Determiner

- Noun: a word that determines the meaning of a noun phrase.
- Noun: a type of prefix.
- Noun: a punctuation mark used to show possession.

An alternative option is to provide different groups with a set of words and ask them to create their own Gobblefunk definitions at home. Mix the children up when they return to school so that each child can test the rest of their group on two or three words.

Board game library

'Perfect family time homework.'

Children benefit hugely from time as a family: discussing, listening and enjoying one another's company. Setting board games for homework not only provides that special family time that all children deserve, but also promotes a range of learning opportunities.

Board games are awash with learning opportunities, as well as encouraging family time and meeting children's competitive urges! New skills and concepts are developed, such as:

- number and shape recognition
- counting and grouping
- reading (initial sounds and words)
- colour recognition
- hand-eye co-ordination
- social skills (waiting, taking turns, sharing)
- verbal communication
- ability to focus and concentrate for sustained periods of time.

Studying, designing and making board games can also be a fantastic DT project. Ask the children to review different board or card games, at home or within school, and write reviews. This can lead to them designing, making and marketing their very own games. Children should consider which age group the game is designed for, what parts are needed, and how they can make it eye-catching. Once the games have been made, they can become a permanent game to play at home, or can go into the board game library of other classrooms.